T0130591

CHANGE THE WORLD USING SOCIAL MEDIA

Library Information Technology Association (LITA) Guides

Marta Mestrovic Deyrup, Ph.D., Acquisitions Editor
Library Information and Technology Association, a division of the American Library Association

The Library Information Technology Association (LITA) Guides provide information and guidance on topics related to cutting edge technology for library and IT specialists.

Written by top professionals in the field of technology, the guides are sought after by librarians wishing to learn a new skill or to become current in today's best practices.

Each book in the series has been overseen editorially since conception by LITA and reviewed by LITA members with special expertise in the specialty area of the book.

Established in 1966, LITA is the division of the American Library Association (ALA) that provides its members and the library and information science community as a whole with a forum for discussion, an environment for learning, and a program for actions on the design, development, and implementation of automated and technological systems in the library and information science field.

Approximately 25 LITA Guides were published by Neal-Schuman and ALA between 2007 and 2015. Rowman & Littlefield took over publication of the series beginning in late 2015. Books in the series published by Rowman & Littlefield are:

Digitizing Flat Media: Principles and Practices
The Librarian's Introduction to Programming Languages
Library Service Design: A LITA Guide to Holistic Assessment, Insight, and Improvement
Data Visualization: A Guide to Visual Storytelling for Librarians
Mobile Technologies in Libraries: A LITA Guide
Innovative LibGuides Applications
Integrating LibGuides into Library Websites
Protecting Patron Privacy: A LITA Guide
The LITA Leadership Guide: The Librarian as Entrepreneur, Leader, and Technologist
Using Social Media to Build Library Communities: A LITA Guide
Managing Library Technology: A LITA Guide
The LITA Guide to No- or Low-Cost Technology Tools for Libraries
Change the World Using Social Media

CHANGE THE WORLD USING SOCIAL MEDIA

Paul Signorelli

ROWMAN & LITTLEFIELD
Lanham • Boulder • New York • London

Published by Rowman & Littlefield
An imprint of The Rowman & Littlefield Publishing Group, Inc.
4501 Forbes Boulevard, Suite 200, Lanham, Maryland 20706
www.rowman.com

6 Tinworth Street, London SE11 5AL, United Kingdom

Change the World Using Social Media is part of the Rowman & Littlefield LITA Guide series. For more information, see https:rowman.com/Action/SE-RIES/RL/LITA.

British Library Cataloguing in Publication Information Available

Library of Congress Cataloging-in-Publication Data

Name: Signorelli, Paul, author.
Title: Change the world using social media / Paul Signorelli.
Description: Lanham : Rowman & Littlefield, [2021] | Series: Library Information Technology Association (LITA) guides | Includes bibliographical references and index. | Summary: "This one-stop handbook to leveraging social media to foster collaboration and achieve positive change uses success stories to illustrate how activists produce transformations in their extended communities"—Provided by publisher.
Identifiers: LCCN 2020035972 (print) | LCCN 2020035973 (ebook) | ISBN 9781538114414 (cloth) | ISBN 9781538114421 (ebook)
Subjects: LCSH: Online social networks—Library applications. | Libraries and community. | Technological innovations—Social aspects. | Social media. | Social change. | Internet and activism.
Classification: LCC Z674.75.S63 S54 2021 (print) | LCC Z674.75.S63 (ebook) | DDC 302.30285—dc23
LC record available at https://lccn.loc.gov/2020035972
LC ebook record available at https://lccn.loc.gov/2020035973

CONTENTS

SPOTLIGHTS

FOREWORD

Maurice Coleman, executive producer and host,
T Is for Training podcast

Creating change is no easy task. It is incredibly difficult to haul yourself to the shore. Transforming into the pebble of change is hard to do. The shore is comfortable, safe. The waters teeming with confusion, strife, and conflict are cold, uninviting, scary, and deeper than you can imagine.

Yet here you are, standing on the shore ready to take that leap. *Change the World Using Social Media* will help you find your depth and make a change.

The social media skills shared in this book will help you become the pebble that creates the change you need to see in your world. These skills and tools are starting points to insightful discussion on creating and sustaining vital and effective communities. *Change the World Using Social Media* will help you find and develop your skills to evaluate if a specific tool is right for your current or future needs.

All social media platforms will connect you and the people next door, just over the hill, across the country, and around the world. *Change the World Using Social Media* will help you seek out those people and communities you want to reach with your message. Social media has the capacity to create vibrant and sustainable communities tied together with powerful connections between individuals who may never meet face-to-face. This book will help you leverage your communities to create positive change.

All social media platforms can nurture, support, and create positive action and instant responses. *Change the World Using Social Media* will help you leverage your network to create decisive action. The book contains interviews with social media practitioners that reveal best practices, lessons learned through success and failure, and the power of a vibrant social network.

The lessons in the book only live on if you have the courage to become the pebble of change.

Be the pebble.

Create waves.

Make a difference.

Change the world.

ACKNOWLEDGMENTS

Numerous people supported completion of this book.

Deepest gratitude to Charles Harmon and Marta Deyrup for initially contacting me about the possibility of writing it. Charles has also been an incredibly patient, supportive, nurturing, and much-appreciated editor throughout the development of the manuscript; he was the person who provided the title and gave me a consistent target toward which I could write. The book wouldn't exist if Charles and Marta hadn't planted the seed.

I am also tremendously grateful to the following people at Rowman & Littlefield: Erinn Slanina, for her always prompt and on-the-mark responses to style questions I had during initial preparation of the manuscript, Kellie Hagan, and everyone else involved in producing the book. They have turned a manuscript into a book and helped it find its audience.

Special thanks to Dan Freeman, who continues to offer me wonderful, much-appreciated opportunities as an instructor and online learning facilitator for the American Library Association (ALA) to develop and facilitate courses innovatively exploring how social media and the development of online communities can foster positive moments in our communities. It was one of those courses that led Marta to contact me with the initial idea for this book.

The book is much richer as a result of the participation of Samantha Adams Becker, Tony Choi, Maurice Coleman, Sam Earp, Jill Hurst-Wahl, David Lee King, Cayden Mak, Jeff Merrell, Elizabeth Myers,

Jonathan Nalder, and Patrick Sweeney—each of whom gave incredible amounts of time and thought to the online, typed-chat interviews that provided original material for *Change the World Using Social Media*. There are also the numerous stories of the activists whose work I included based on their own social media presence, numerous online resources detailing their work, and the writing (e.g., books and articles) they have produced or that include summaries of their work; the examples they provide served as continuous inspiration as I wrote *Change the World*. This, of course, leads to an acknowledgment of the work produced by dozens of writers who provided a tremendous amount of useful and inspiring background information during the research for and writing of *Change the World Using Social Media* and, I hope, will make the book part of a global discussion.

I can't say enough in describing the gratitude I feel for family members (particularly Licia, my father, and Carol), friends, and colleagues who kept asking when the book would be ready so they could read it. (Don't let anyone fool you: the interest expressed by and the support of readers is a highly motivating factor for writers.) I also received incalculable support from members of my professional "families" in ALA, ATD, #etmooc (Alec Couros and all our co-conspirators in learning), ShapingEDU, and *T Is for Training*; learners with whom I work and interact, often long after formal courses come to an end; and current and retired colleagues from the San Francisco Public Library system.

Andy Foote, James Ouyang, and other members of a San Francisco–based gaming community who introduced me to Slack and patiently engaged in numerous conversations about online collaboration, social media, and activism contributed more than they will ever know to the content of this book and the work that I do in nurturing and facilitating online communities.

Heartfelt thanks, everyone. You are among the wonderful pebbles that Maurice Coleman lovingly describes and honors in the foreword to this book.

PREFACE

PURPOSE

Welcome to *Change the World Using Social Media*—a book designed to help you think about—and rethink—how social media platforms can improve your ability to engage, inspire, and collaborate with current and prospective supporters to produce positive change within the onsite and online communities you serve. I am not going to tell you that you must use specific tools (e.g., Facebook, Instagram, Snapchat, or Twitter). I believe you can best make those choices based on how effectively a social media tool allows you to accomplish something you haven't been able to accomplish to your satisfaction up to this point. I hope, instead, to help you understand how a variety of social media tools work and how your change-the-world colleagues are using them as part of their overall tool kits to produce positive results.

The book consistently shows you that social media functions through a dynamic, ever-changing blend of online and—yes—onsite resources that often evolve beyond the uses imagined by those who created them. It accepts that the ways those tools work day-to-day undergo subtle—and sometimes not-so-subtle—changes in ways you might not even notice unless you read the overly long and turgidly written user agreements foisted upon you by those who design, provide, and update the tools. *Change the World*, furthermore, is meant to help you see that your positive and negative perceptions regarding those tools can quickly change. What appears to be great one day can fall from favor overnight through the experiences you have online and as news reports, articles, books, and online commentary on how those tools are used cause you and many others to seek alternative social media resources—or, at the very least, reduce your presence on those platforms until something else draws you back.

AN AUDIENCE OF ACTIVISTS

The word *activist* is one I use often throughout this book with the belief that it is well past the time when "activists" should be thought of only as those people you see in mainstream media reports or encounter in onsite and online protest movements. Activists, in our time, are those who use the tools available to them online and onsite to foster the changes they want to see as they work toward the ever-elusive goal of creating the world of their dreams. They don't necessarily "start out wanting to change the world," suggests *T Is for Training* podcast executive producer and host, Maurice Coleman. "They usually start out wanting to change this . . . that one situation."[1] In these terms, activists work in a variety of settings—some highly visible, some not at all visible to the average person—but what is important is the way those settings affect you and those around you in ways to which you generally aren't inclined to give much attention.

If you are aware of what is happening around you—locally, regionally, nationally, and/or internationally—and if you are looking for ways to change what you don't like in that landscape, you are, potentially, an activist, and you should find inspiration and useful tips from those you encounter here. If you are interested in knowing more about how social media tools can help you produce the positive, small- and large-scale changes you envision, this book is for you.

SCOPE AND RANGE OF SUBJECTS COVERED

For the most part, I avoid lengthy discussions here involving theoretical approaches to and the underpinnings of social media and activism; instead, I offer stories from and about activists incorporating social media into their overall efforts. What you will find here are examples and ideas—some familiar, some collected through the series of personal interviews I conducted with friends and colleagues who creatively approach social media as one way of achieving their goals. There is a strong focus on some of the social media platforms (e.g., Facebook, Instagram, LinkedIn, Snapchat, Twitter, and YouTube) that are used by the largest number of people in the United States and globally; on some of the types of social media platforms (e.g., blogging, videoconferencing, and collaboration tools) that can help you in your change-the-world efforts; and on platforms (e.g., Zoom and Slack) that are social but not necessarily acknowledged universally as social media tools. (For a glimpse of how expansive the social media environment is, skim the list of more than 100 sites on Wikipedia's "List of Social Networking Websites" page.[2])

This book very much draws upon my perspective and experience as a teacher-trainer-learner-doer working onsite and online; as an onsite and online facilitator in learning and other environments; as an organizer of onsite and online communities; as an active participant in and contributor to a variety of communities that seamlessly interweave interactions onsite and online; and as someone who loves learning by example and through immersion. What I have attempted to do is provide you access to unsung heroes in activism while also exploring the stories of some well-known activists.

You will, throughout *Change the World*, find short sections interwoven with the main text to provide tips on how to approach the platforms and types of social media tools discussed. You will also find short lists selected from the numerous resources you can use to further develop your understanding of and ability to incorporate the tools and actions explored. All of this is designed to stimulate thought and conversations that lead to actions and results you might not otherwise have produced.

EXPERIENCE AND APPROACH

My initial reactions to social media were not positive. The tools I was hearing about during the first decade of the twenty-first century seemed to have little application to any work in which I was involved, so I approached them with a great deal of reluctance and skepticism. As friends and colleagues introduced me to a few of them, I began halfheartedly exploring what they could do—beginning with LinkedIn, then turning to WordPress for blogging, slowly moving onto Twitter *a few years later* (no, I wasn't at that point anywhere close to being an early adaptor), and very reluctantly joining Facebook when Dan Freeman, a much-appreciated friend and colleague in the American Library Association, offered me a chance to teach an online introduction to social media course—but only if I would include Facebook as one of the platforms covered in the course. (To this day, I have tremendously mixed feelings about Facebook. I am there primarily because so many people with whom I want and need to stay in contact are there. I'm not particularly enamored of the way Facebook algorithms promote or bury posts, potentially leaving you with the mistaken belief that you are reaching far more people than you actually are,[3] but I also do appreciate the way it allows me to learn from colleagues through the links they share and the observations they post.)

A turning point came for me when a colleague who was a Twitter afficionado badgered me into trying the platform. When I stumbled upon tweet chats—live, well-facilitated discussions that in the best of situations bring global communities together for lively, rapid-paced, inspirational interactions—I was completely hooked; the sense of community and the recognition of possibilities for positive results from those online conversations rivaled anything I was experiencing in face-to-face settings.

Designing and facilitating webinars, online workshops, and courses—along with engaging as a learner in highly interactive, massive, open online courses—continues to shape the way I approach training-teaching-learning. More importantly, it continues to provide opportunities for me to see how social media tools can be an engaging and productive part of any effort to collaborate in small- and large-scale efforts to foster transformation—which, after all, is at the heart of the best learning opportunities. Incorporating the positive use of social media tools into other collaboration situations—working with colleagues to help rebuild a struggling chapter of a national training organization; working with teachers, trainers, and learners to incorporate educational technology into learning efforts that support organizational goals; and drawing colleagues together to plan and implement initiatives designed to improve the situations of members of the communities we serve—provides opportunities that would otherwise not have been available.

Reading and adapting what you find in *Change the World Using Social Media* should provide similar inspiration and opportunities for you too.

All too often, social media advocates create an unrealistic vision—both positive and negative—of what you can expect if you decide to incorporate social media tools into your efforts to produce positive change. Throughout *Change the World*, I focus on what I believe are efforts to successfully promote positive change (e.g., make communities safer, more habitable, more welcoming, and more equitable for everyone) through blended (onsite and online) social movements including #BlackLivesMatter, #ClimateStrike/#FridaysForFuture, #MarchForOur-Lives/#NeverAgain, #MeToo, and #WomensMarch. I explore efforts that design, provide, and promote lifelong learning opportunities that help employees develop and maintain the skills needed to assure that they and the businesses, organizations, customers, and clients they serve will thrive in an ever-changing economy and world. (Examples include the #ShapingEDU initiative[4] through Arizona State University, designed to shape the future of learning in the digital age, and #etmooc,[5] the Educational Technology & Media massive open online course whose participants unexpectedly transformed it from its initial design of being a free, ten-week, global online course into becoming a highly engaged community of learning with core participants who were still occasionally meeting and collaborating online through social media platforms seven years after the "ten-week" course formally concluded). And I also call attention to individual efforts by people you might not initially be inclined to think of as activists, e.g., those involved in teaching, workplace learning, librarianship, and fundraising.

By the time you finish reading and begin using this book in your change-the-world efforts, you should have a good understanding of what social media might—and might not—do to support your work. You should have plenty of examples about how to effectively incorporate social media tools into your efforts. And you should have lots of ideas regarding how you can continue to learn about and adopt new social media tools you encounter.

With that in mind, here's what you can expect.

CHAPTER-BY-CHAPTER ORGANIZATION AND CONTENT DESCRIPTIONS

Chapter 1 explores key aspects of how to utilize social media tools available to you, begins looking at ways to immediately incorporate social media into the work you are doing, and reviews when you might—and might not—want to use social media to work with your colleagues and supporters.

Chapter 2, with a focus on Facebook, explores how that platform (at its best) can quickly and effectively put you in contact with colleagues all over the world, while (at its worst) leaving you with the mistaken impression that you are reaching far more people than you are actually reaching, and can marginalize communities and individuals most in need of reaching others to achieve positive social change. You will see how others have used Facebook to foster small- and large-scale positive social change—at times in ways far beyond anything they could have imagined.

Chapter 3 turns to Twitter to show how this platform, with its 280-character limit per post, can connect you to colleagues and supporters globally at a variety of levels, allowing you to view content without responding or, at the opposite end of the spectrum of levels of engagement, conduct transformative in-the-moment conversations through your tweets. You will also see how the use of carefully chosen keywords (hashtags), sessions involving conversation-by-Twitter, and backchannels (online conversations, via Twitter, that extend the reach of onsite and online activities) can be part of your overall effort to foster positive change.

Chapter 4 focuses on LinkedIn and other social networking tools created primarily to foster connections and conversations between business colleagues and between employers and prospective employees. The chapter suggests that although these tools remain tremendously underutilized by those interested in drawing upon the skills and resources of their business colleagues in their efforts to foster positive social change, these tools can increase your ability to effectively engage and communicate with business colleagues who might also be interested in the work you do.

Chapter 5 turns to Snapchat, Instagram, and Flickr, the popular image-centric social media platforms available to you to reach your colleagues and supporters with compelling photographs and brief, engaging bits of text designed to inspire positive action. In this chapter, you will see how activists addressing a variety of challenges and issues are incorporating those tools into their change-the-world tool kits.

Chapter 6 explores blogging as a key pathway to sharing your story with current and prospective members of your community. It helps you understand how the combination of text, images, videos, and links to useful and inspiring resources helps you engage and motivate your colleagues and supporters.

Chapter 7 demonstrates how incorporating videos and podcasts into your work can be far simpler than you might initially imagine, and how that action can open up new forms of expression for you to use in engaging your current and prospective partners in fostering positive social change. The chapter includes examples of how activists are incorporating YouTube and podcasting platforms into their change-the-world tool kit.

Chapter 8 focuses on the use of social media videoconferencing tools to create a sense of physical presence—telepresence—among participants that erases geographic barriers and helps you understand that "face-to-face" interactions happen online too. It shows that, when used effectively, these aids to fostering telepresence create the sense that members of geographically separated communities are working collaboratively, face-to-face, in ways that strengthen community members' ability to meet, plan, and act to change the world using social media.

Chapter 9 explores how online fundraising platforms including GoFundMe are, when used successfully, raising billions of dollars for small- and large-scale initiatives designed to make positive changes for individuals and communities throughout the world.

Chapter 10 turns to a difficult topic: how the use of social media tools to foster positive change will spur opposition at a variety of levels—the worst of which includes trolling, intentionally cruel levels of harassment, and fake news posts designed to damage your positive reputation and hinder your ability to continue the work you are doing. The chapter explores how trolls and others engaged in online harassment have affected others engaged in small- and large-scale community-based efforts, and the steps activists have taken to avoid being overwhelmed by those extreme challenges.

Chapter 11, connecting themes and examples developed throughout the book, reminds you that successfully incorporating social media tools into your work involves much more than simply posting and then waiting for results. The same strong organizational skills required for any change-the-world effort apply here. This chapter explores how activists combine strong organizational skills with collaborations that flow seamlessly between onsite and online settings to produce positive results, and leaves you with a reminder that engaging successfully via social media tools means you are never alone in the work you are doing.

BEYOND THE BOOK: SPECIAL FEATURES

Reading a book, for me, parallels any other learning opportunity I accept: the more I bring to the act of reading, and the more I quickly adopt and adapt what I am reading, the more positive the results I see. While participating in a massive open online course designed as a weeks-long exploration of and discussion about one book (*The Innovator's Mindset: Empower Learning, Unleash Talent, and Lead a Culture of Creativity*,[6] by George Couros) in 2018, I realized that I was actually changing the way I read as a result of my participation in Couros's course. Because the course centered on the content of the book and discussions around that content, I was reading a few chapters each week to prepare for the online discussions that extended into tweeting, blogging, and engaging in other activities on social media platforms. But because I had read parts of the book before joining the course, I took a different, more relaxed approach to "reading": when I came across a link to an article, a blog post, or a video that Couros was citing, I frequently set the book aside, found the cited resource online, and read or viewed it before returning to the next sentence of the book. The result was twofold: I had a much deeper, more transformative—and much longer—reading experience, and I realized that "reading," for anyone with access to online resources, is changing, in important ways, what a twenty-first-century book can be. Reading is just as much what is beyond the covers and incorporated into my reading experience as what is contained within the covers (physical or, in the case of ebooks, virtual).[7]

Change the World Using Social Media is designed to operate at multiple levels. You can read what is within the covers and walk away with what you need to know. You can expand the book—and your knowledge and understanding of the topic—by following links contained within the endnotes. You can find additional content—developed for but not included in the print or ebook editions—including full, lightly edited transcripts of some of the interviews used for this book on my *Building Creative Bridges* blog and tagged with the title of this book.[8] And you can add to the content itself by engaging with other readers through the online "ChangeTheWorld-Co" community on Slack to extend the conversations I hope the book inspires. To join that community, please contact me directly at paul@paulsignorelli.com and include a brief (one-line) description of your interest in learning more about using social media to change the world.

Thanks for taking the time to read the book, and thanks in advance for any contributions you decide to make through participation in the *Change the World* Slack community and other online platforms.

I

WHAT IS SOCIAL MEDIA AND WHAT CAN IT DO FOR YOU?

Social media is one of many tools available to you as you promote positive social change. At its best, it involves high levels of engagement; an ever-shifting set of skills; an understanding of how change occurs; and a commitment to transparency, listening, and responding civilly. This chapter explores key aspects of how to utilize the tools available to you and begins looking at ways to immediately incorporate social media into the work you are doing.

Change often starts small, with the simplest, most innocuous of actions. For me, it was a reaction to the news that a Minneapolis Public Schools administrator, DeRay Mckesson, had driven from Minneapolis to Ferguson to witness and document what was happening in Ferguson in the aftermath of the shooting of Michael Brown by a member of the Ferguson Police Department. I had been reading about the shootings of fellow citizens who were African American—shot by members of police departments and by private citizens who felt threatened by the presence of young men like Trayvon Martin because those citizens were Black. I was—and continue to be—increasingly horrified by what I was and am seeing in "post-racial" America.

When Mckesson began reporting from Ferguson, via Twitter, I recognized that something had changed significantly. In addition to all the other forms of media that provided first-rate, reliable information about critically important issues, social media seemed to provide an ever-increasing level of access to and potential for involvement in defining, reacting to, and seeking information about issues and solutions to those issues. This was raw and visceral—far beyond the polished, often pseudo-objective reporting that comes from the mainstream-media representatives whose work I admire and devour. I was experiencing and willingly joining multi-level, non-curated, expansive reports and conversations and calls to action through Twitter, Facebook, blogs, podcasts, and other online resources. Social media was not completely replacing one-way broadcast media including newspaper, radio, and television as important, significant, much-needed primary sources of information; those resources remain the meat and potatoes of information gathering at a time when I struggle to distinguish between fake news and reliable reporting. On the other hand, social media tools were increasingly adding an important, dynamic, potentially world-changing element to my conversations and perceptions about the world, how my colleagues and I interact with it, and how I might attempt to work with others to change it in positive ways.

If you are already familiar with Twitter and other social media platforms, you need only glance at the most cursory list of hashtags to become aware of the scope—and tenor, both positive and negative—of conversations and the way that the use of hashtags is making action-based conversation easier for even the most inexperienced of activists. Examples include #ArabSpring, #BlackLivesMatter, #Brexit, #BringBackOurGirls, #ClimateStrike/FridaysForFuture, #DACA, #Dreamers, #Ferguson, #GunSense, #HealthReform, #MAGA, #MarchForOurLives/#NeverAgain/#VoteForOurLives, #MeToo, #NODAPL, #NotOneMore, #NotInOurName, #OccupyWallStreet, and #ParisAccord.

Make no mistake about it: this is a deeply personal, highly transformative level of change for someone incorporating social media into a change-the-world tool kit. It began changing the way I used and viewed social media tools including Facebook and Twitter. I began initiating conversations that I previously had thought of as being too risky for online; my shift came out of a decision that avoiding those online conversations that exposed and forced me to confront some of the deepest differences I have and see with friends and colleagues was far more risky than not acknowledging and confronting them. I began and continue to openly reach out to those whose experiences and political beliefs differ tremendously from my own. I sought to listen, to learn, to find common ground—just as they did, with the same spirit of collegiality—and attempt to produce positive change in response to the difficult and often painful challenges that so often seemed to irrevocably separate us.

At times, my own tongue-in-cheek approach (e.g., creating and promoting the use of the hashtag #MakeAmericaCivilAgain in response to the disgustingly uncivil nature of discourse displayed during the 2016 US presidential election) produced surprisingly encouraging results: my colleagues and I manage, at times, to find common ground in the idea that promoting civility in our interactions is an important and productive first step in addressing some of our most wicked problems. We also realize that incorporating humor into our discussion is an important element in trying to recivilize our exchanges.

I am drawn into these conversations—as I hope you are or will be—and I am engaged by small- and large-scale desires to positively respond to the challenges faced by members of a variety of local, regional, national, and global communities, because I believe in the power of activism grounded in civility. The use of social media tools is one of many resources you have in your personal and collaborative tool kit; the people you will encounter in this book know and understand this because they use social media nearly every day.

Some (e.g., Samantha Adams Becker, Maurice Coleman, Jill Hurst-Wahl, David Lee King, Jeff Merrell, Jonathan Nalder, and Patrick Sweeney) have been friends and colleagues for many years and are people who, before they agreed to be interviewed for this book, did not overtly identify themselves as activists. The fact that they—as librarians, educators, and writers—foster social change at small- and large-scale levels through their activity in a variety of social media platforms, will, I hope, encourage you to see that you don't need to be famous or have thousands of followers in your social media accounts to be able to contribute to positive change in the communities you serve. Others (e.g., Elizabeth Myers and Cayden Mak) have titles and responsibilities that put them at the heart of facilitating positive change within their communities. They are people I came to know through the use of social media and other online resources as I was seeking activists with diverse backgrounds who use social media effectively in a variety of environments and cover a wide range of issues that attract the effort of activists fostering positive social change. And there are, of course, the well-known activists whom I have never met face-to-face, but feel as if I know because of the levels of engagement they inspire through their social media presence.

Regardless of the levels of your current use of social media and your reach in promoting change, you will find plenty of examples here to help you see how social media, as part of your overall activist's tool kit, can provide opportunities for conversation, planning, collaboration, and action that will bring you and others closer to riding waves of change rather than being drowned by them. You'll also encounter plenty of examples of how some of your most creative colleagues using social media remain committed to honestly and openly cultivating a sense of trust and engagement with their online and onsite collaborators and those they serve.

Cayden Mak, Executive Director of 18 Million Rising, spoke on this during our initial interview for this book:

> I think it's not a coincidence that our staff still tends to be highly educated—not just in a book/academic way—but many of them, past and present, have been schooled so to speak in the history of social movements and stuff like that. That kind of expertise allows us to speak from a very genuine place—I think the voice and the tone that we built was intentionally comradely in that way because we share a set of cultural references, but we're interested in bringing more people on board with those cultural references. I think it's been a careful effort to ensure that we both demonstrate our expertise while making that accessible to people.
>
> The thing that this process taught me is the importance of trust. With other organizing formations I was a part of at the time, we were building trust in order to do high-stakes things like shutting down New York State Assembly meetings and risking arrest in order to highlight hypocrisy in the university system. Online, there isn't necessarily a sense that there are high-risk actions to take. However, I think online organizers often do themselves a disservice when they emphasize that their tools and platforms make social action "easy" or "simple." Because the whole point of organizing, to me, whether it's online or off, is to build trust among a group of people in order for them to take calculated risks towards a goal.[1]

———*૦/*૦/*૦———

The Importance of Engagement in Social Media and Change
Maurice Coleman, Harford County Public Library Tech Trainer

Engagement is asking the question of your people—"people" being your followers. "What do you think about X, and why?" . . . "How can we help you today and tomorrow?" Questions sometimes leading to dialogue. That seems to me to be engagement: having a conversation with your followers. That is engagement.

Be genuine and honest. Make sure they are who they say they are. If you are in a deep conversation with someone, seek to take it to email, phone, or face-to-face for more thought-out and contemplative conversation. Don't make everything public. That is for your protection and the protection of the person you are talking to. Seek some sort of private conversation on sensitive topics. You can use social media to get your foot in the door. You don't have to use it as the only way to communicate with someone. Be as concise as possible without losing the meaning of your words.

———*૦/*૦/*૦———

ELEMENTS OF SOCIAL MEDIA

Attempting to define social media can be challenging because some tools are clearly part of your social media landscape, while others appear to be designed for and directed toward use in businesses or other settings. Contributors to Wikipedia suggest the term encompasses "interactive computer-mediated technologies that facilitate the creation or sharing of information, ideas, career interests and other forms of expression via virtual communities and networks."[2] This puts platforms including Facebook, Instagram, LinkedIn, Snapchat, Twitter, and You-Tube into your social media landscape, but leaves business/enterprise-level platforms such as Slack in a potentially gray area. I consistently, throughout this book, include any collaboration tools I have seen used by online communities sharing thoughts and working together toward a shared social goal.

A transformative moment occurs the first time you see your thoughts and your work shared by someone else on Facebook, retweeted, or in some other way extended to friends of friends, acquaintances, and, most importantly of all, to people you would otherwise not have encountered. To see a "like" on Facebook, a heart on Twitter, or any other symbol of positive acknowledgment invariably offers a jolt of pleasure at an emotional and physiological level.[3] It is an initial reminder that this is far different than writing a letter or sending an email to an individual. Social media is potentially far more dynamic than posting information in a printed or online newsletter, and it delivers responses much faster, more dynamically, and in potentially more transformative ways than anything a letter to the editor of a newspaper ever could have produced.

The moment, however, is a small or potentially large missed opportunity if you do nothing more than bask in the brief burst of pleasure the response provides, for you have missed a key element of social media that is so obvious it's almost silly to have to mention it: It. Is. Social. This means you have to quickly move past the build-it-and-they-will-come approach; you have to watch for the responses to your online work, respond to those responses, and work diligently to engage rather than broadcast—never losing sight of the fact that you need to bring all your organizational skills to this endeavor and remember that social media is part of your overall change-the-world landscape, not something that operates and produces results in a vacuum.

A second key element, therefore, is the use of social media tools as an invitation to engage and cultivate engagement; engagement, after all, is a critically important part of trying to change the world, or anything else, in positive ways through social media and the other resources you have as a current or potential activist. This quickly became obvious to me when I moved heavily into blogging about some of the changes that were and are taking place in my lifelong-learning environment and helping reshape the way my learners—my co-conspirators in learning—and I learn and use what we learn. When I blog about a book or article highlighting a development or trend of interest to colleagues, I often mention the blog post in a separate post on LinkedIn, Twitter, and Facebook; by including a mention of the author of the book or article, I gain the attention of those authors and, at the very least, attract responses expressing appreciation. The rewarding payoff, however, comes when I write a follow-up to that person on the same platform (e.g., LinkedIn, Twitter, or Facebook). Suddenly and frequently, a random post morphs into the beginning of a conversation. Some of those conversations lead to exchanges extending over months or years; informal and formal collaborations extending the work that drew us into our initial conversation; and friendships that start in those online settings and extend into face-to-face encounters at conferences and other professional gatherings as well as in other online communities beyond the ones that provided an initial, tentative connection.

This form of extended conversation highlights a third often overlooked element of social media: at its most highly nuanced and sophisticated levels, it transcends the bounds of time and space in ways not previously possible. There is the synchronous side of social media that is immediately obvious: I post something, you immediately respond, I respond in kind, and the conversation grows in a real-time moment. A less-obvious side involves the amount of actual time that can pass between contributions to and extensions of that in-the-moment conversation. For example, I post something today, you see it a couple of days from now and respond, a week or two later I respond, and this extended, continuous "moment" of conversation can last for weeks, months, or years if we are obsessive and diligent enough to continue exploring and addressing the topic that initially drew us together. It clearly doesn't matter whether you and I are physically sitting in the same room while the conversation takes place or are separated by hundreds or thousands of miles; as long as we both keep the moment going, the exchange has a uniquely online life that continues to produce results online and onsite as long as we nourish it and act upon what we are considering. (You'll find a detailed exploration of this theme, within the context of learning, in Pekka Ihanainen and John Moravec's "Pointillist, Cyclical, and Overlapping: Multidimensional Facets of Time in Online Learning,"[4] which very much helped me develop my own understanding of how extended asynchronous online conversations can help produce positive results.[5])

The Role of Passion in Social Media and Change
Samantha Adams Becker, ShapingEDU community facilitator

Social change requires passion. Passion is the flame that ignites action. Indifference causes stagnant activity. Voices and content that clearly come from a place of genuine conviction and empathy pull you in with a stronger magnetic force. There is also a sense of honesty behind passion—you can see through a person or organization to their cause. But there's also a danger because passion is something that can easily be faked through carefully crafted content—or well-trained public speaking. Passion, without altruism, can go really wrong. Or it can be unintentionally misdirected and lead people down the wrong road. Passion must meet a great deal of thought, planning, and taking into consideration the impact on people.

No matter how much situations or times seem desperately challenging and impossible to fix, I believe that people have the power to change the world. It starts with an idea, then authentic conversation and discourse, and then strategy, and then action.

I believe in being a dreamer and a doer—brainstorming ideas for change and then being able to execute on them. Dreams die unless you nurture them and make them real. So a passion is dormant unless you share it, water it, and actively help it grow. No one is going to do that for you. You have to do it yourself. And once you know how to do it yourself, you can better teach others to do the same—but enable them to flourish in their own unique ways.

At the end of the day, all I care about is helping people. First, my family (and my closest friends—who are family), and then everyone else. Even those I disagree with. Kindness and education are my two passions.

—⟊⟊⟊—

A fourth key element worth mentioning here is that social media can be messy and expansive rather than orderly and in any way controlled by those engaged in its use. This became obvious to me when I joined an online learning community of approximately 1,500 learners engaged initially in a ten-week massive open online course designed to explore the use of technology in education (#etmooc, the Educational Technology & Media MOOC) in early 2013. We learned by doing, which meant we used educational technology to meet in highly interactive online learning sessions each week; extended our work and conversations over multiple platforms including Google Hangouts, Twitter, YouTube, and blogs; and carried our conversations into a larger world via social media that brought unexpected guests—some of the people whose work we

were studying—into our learning conversations. When the course formally concluded at the end of our tenth week together, the conversations and learning (and small-scale activism) didn't. One member of the
learning community jokingly posted a tweet saying the course wasn't
over until we said it was over; the result was that a small group of us
continue to meet to this day online to continue our conversations. The
social-change aspect of our work is subtle, but significant: we are still
applying what we learned (and continue to learn together) in ways that
are changing the face of learning in positive ways among the various
communities we serve. A key point made repeatedly in our early days
together was that not everyone would see everything produced by
members of this online community of educators-as-activists—the range
of platforms was too large and the content too broad to be completely
absorbed by any single member. But by choosing to absorb and apply
what served each of us, we continue to contribute to positive changes in
our community (and communities) globally while recognizing that some
of us will never see or even be aware of the impact our collaborations
produce.

It is well worth noting that there are times when you might not feel
safe or comfortable incorporating social media tools into your work, as
Sam Earp, Christian Resource Ministry[6] Director of Development for
the Middle East, says:

> We do not use Facebook, as it is too traceable . . . let me rethink that.
> We do use Facebook for those already in [a] relationship with us. We
> do not use it as the first point of contact. An example: A young family
> using an in-country application found a distribution point for food
> [and] hygiene items, etc. She came to ask for help [and] received it.
> Over the course of time, she has become a major leader in the efforts
> we are making toward refugees. She is currently training about six
> other women to assist her in further expanding the efforts. One ele-
> ment of social change this produces is the liberation of women into
> leadership roles which become acceptable to the male dominated
> social environment.
>
>   Our organization is Christian value-based, which is forbidden in
> some of the Middle Eastern countries. Lebanon is the only country
> where Christian work and Christianity is acceptable, even though the
> country is governed by Hezbollah. At one time, the country was 65
> percent Christian, and Muslims were the minority. That is now re-

versed. The more fundamental the society in its religious heritage, the more difficult and dangerous it can be even to help with compassion relief. Social media is easily traceable, as most Middle Eastern government[s] keep tight controls on its use. In North Africa, where I was working in the late Fall (2017), [they] complete[ly] closed down Internet usage for three days! With such tight controls on accessibility, social media cannot be the main or dependable source for any change.[7]

Social media is not a primary way Earp and the Ministry reach those they are trying to serve. As you consider using social media to promote social change, you can learn from what Earp has described—in spite of all you are hearing and reading about Twitter, Facebook, and other online platforms supporting social change, there are times when the danger makes the use of these tools ill-advised, if not outright foolish. The reverse side of that, of course, is that there are times when social media does help you—as it helps Earp and those he serves—to support others and foster some level of social change. This generally occurs once a relationship is in place and trust has been established.

SOCIAL MEDIA IN OUR LARGER WORLD OF CHANGE

You probably carry a number of assumptions about the role social media plays in activism, so it is well worth questioning those assumptions as you read this book so you avoid overestimating the role social media can play in your efforts. Among those assumptions (drawn from numerous media accounts) is that social media by itself creates enormous social change—as many people believe it did through use of Twitter and Facebook in 2011 during the Arab Spring, its Spanish counterpart (the Indignados gatherings), and Occupy Wall Street and its various offshoots (and, more recently, through #BlackLivesMatter, #Climate-Strike/#FridaysForFuture, #MarchForOurLives/#NeverAgain, and #MeToo).

Paolo Gerbaudo's wonderfully nuanced, research-based examination of the role social media played in the first three movements I cited here suggests a different picture. In *Tweets and the Streets: Social Media and Contemporary Activism*,[8] Gerbaudo places great emphasis on social media as a way of organizing communities so they can meet in physical locations that become the focal point of their efforts to foster social change. In each of the three case studies he presents, he shows how social media played important roles in the weeks and months leading up to the blossoming of *onsite* activities in settings that became the iconic representations of the movements (as Zuccotti Park in New York became for the Occupy movement). He consistently quotes those active in the three movements to call attention to social media as a tool used to fashion what he calls "a choreography of assembly." He provides plenty of evidence showing—particularly in the case of the Occupy movement—that initial online efforts to foster social change evolved tremendously and positively once the movements had physical sites to which their activities and efforts could draw attention from others, including mainstream media representatives who were slow to pay attention until the movements offered a physical manifestation they could cover.

———

The Intersection of Social Media, Economics, and the Commons
Cayden Mak

A lot of my thinking about social media is informed by the way I see it influencing the economy—a lot of the big social media companies are these firms that started with a vague idea that they wanted to build something to connect people, and as they struggle to figure out how to make money, their technology becomes more and more coercive. I think that's a big challenge because they do have some value and have been helpful in a variety of contexts—like bringing social movements from different corners of society into the attention of "the mainstream"—but they're building this hyper-surveilled social space that is also completely enclosed. It feels like there's no such thing as the commons anymore, and that's partially because social media has become the biggest "third space" for most young people. I think it's a problem also because they have taken up so much bandwidth (literally and figuratively) that they have become the whole Internet for some people. I think that's scary, especially in light of our current debate about net neutrality—we're stuck on the ISP level and need to also talk about the platform/gateway/software level.

Social media is powerful because of its network effects, but I worry about monopolization, or even just dependence on a corporate platform to communicate as an individual or small group online.

—⟨♥♥♥⟩—

What has obviously continued to evolve during the time that has passed since Gerbaudo published *Tweets and the Streets* is that social change doesn't always come overtly and visibly through those large-scale onsite manifestations of a movement; a community such as #etmooc can foster slow, long-term transformation through its online interactions that eventually filter out globally as individual members of that community, step by step, change the way they work onsite as well as online; inspire, by example, the diffusion of the change they are fostering; and document through the use of social media platforms and more traditional means (e.g., peer-reviewed papers) the positive results they are producing so that others adapt those changes and eventually produce equally positive results.

Returning six years later to the landscape similar to and at times overlapping with that explored in *Tweets and the Streets*, Zeynep Tufekci provides you (in her book *Twitter and Tear Gas: The Power and Fragility of Networked Protest*[9]) with a first-rate survey that not only recognizes the importance of online communities and their relationships to their onsite counterparts, but consistently explores the challenges of and need for engaging in long-term efforts to develop strong organizational infrastructures—a theme more fully reviewed in the final chapter of *Change the World*. Her third chapter ("Leading the Leaderless"), in particular, is a primer not to be ignored if you want guidance on what happens when online communities fail to work, over a long period of time, to build sustainable organizational structures.

—⟨♥♥♥⟩—

Pro Tips: Social Media

"There is power in connecting people who may [be] in the same situation and have the same feelings about it. Fostering genuine conversations can lead to organized action." —Samantha Adams Becker, whose work with the New Media Consortium (NMC), ShapingEDU initiative, and other organizations incorporates the use of social media into fostering positive change.

"If you are experimenting [with social media], then don't think it has to be perfect. If it is part of your organizational/corporate plan, then consider what guidelines you have for other forms of corporate communication and how they may or may not apply to 'social media.' Use it to engage and inform and have some damn fun." —Maurice Coleman, whose biweekly *T Is for Training* podcast draws together trainer-teacher-learner-doers fostering change through educational offerings in libraries

"The connections you make on social media mirror those in your physical world. They don't end with a screen; they're part of you, an extension." —Elizabeth Myers, who uses social media tools to foster community engagement through her work as the community librarian for Markham Public Library (Ontario, Canada)

"For me, it has to begin with starting conversations—not 'telling' as much as sparking curiosity and social, back-and-forth response. So not just putting info and ideas out there, but having follow-up spaces for people to chat more *and* also being in others' lives and supporting their conversations." —Jonathan Nalder, whose global work through Future-We (based in Brisbane, Australia) incorporates social media tools into efforts to prepare learners for success in an ever-evolving global environment

———

On the other hand, what you see as you immerse yourself in a study of the blending of online and onsite change-the-world efforts is the speed with which social media can mobilize people to take positive action without ever becoming part of the kind of onsite communities mobilized through the Arab Spring, the Spanish Indignados, and Occupy Wall Street, as Samantha Adams Becker (president of SAB Creative and Consulting and one of the community organizers for the ShapingE-DU initiative through Arizona State University) noted in an interview for this book:

For me, personally, when the first travel ban was implemented by the US government in early 2017, I witnessed how powerful organizations like ACLU [the American Civil Liberties Union] became because it was easy to disseminate information about how to help and where to go to help people impacted. They were able to raise a lot of money and recruit volunteers very quickly.

The takeaway is that one individual or one organization can make a difference. By sharing your voice, it can resonate with so many people who will then rally behind you. The power of one multiplies . . . to infinity.

In education, perhaps a more passive but also important form of social change has materialized on Twitter. Education leaders and practitioners come together from different backgrounds, institutions, [and] parts of the world to discuss their experiences with major challenges, major success stories, etc. Scaling solutions requires this kind of cross-institution and cross-culture sharing.

Social media enables continuous sharing and encourages people to connect through their experiences, whether it's sharing educational resources, posing thought-provoking questions, or meeting new people that become instrumental in helping you build a project/ initiative. In that sense, it is both a learning and career development vehicle.[10]

All of this leads, in the next section, to a brief examination of how change occurs and how it can be fostered through the use of social media tools as part of your overall activist's tool kit.

FACILITATING CHANGE

The theory is hardly new even if the tools available to you are—and it's probably safe to say that you haven't yet seen the last of the social media tools that will change the way you work. If you look back to any of the numerous resources available to you on the topic of how change is fostered, you put yourself in a strong position to apply long-proven techniques to contemporary efforts incorporating ever-changing social media tools.

If you peruse the fifth edition of the seminal book *Diffusion of Innovations*[11] originally published in 1962, for example, you absorb numerous examples from Everett Rogers regarding how those serving as activists in a variety of settings have successfully facilitated change. Rogers leads you through five categories describing those involved in various stages of the change process: the "Innovators" who create something new; the small group of "Early Adopters" that first begins spreading the change; the "Early Majority" that through deliberation pushes the proposed change toward widespread adoption; the skeptical "Late Majority" that accepts the widespread adoption; and the "Laggards" who never will adopt the change. Rogers, writing in a pre-social-media age, shows you how "diffusion networks" have, throughout history, come together in a variety of ways—including through the actions of those who, because of the positions they hold within communities and organizations, are able to serve as positive sponsors to and advocates for the proposed change. (You know who they are in your own life; some of them may have inspired you to become interested in using social media to promote the positive changes you hope to foster within your communities.) Most importantly, Rogers helps you understand that successful efforts at change rely heavily on adoption by people who learn about and embrace the proposed change because someone they know and trust embraced it first.

This has tremendous repercussions for you as you incorporate social media into your efforts to foster positive social change. Recognizing that this is still very much a process of building trust and nurturing effective communication, you begin to see that the same social approach used in creating sustainable communities of change through leading by example, as well as by overt advocacy, works with social media, just as it works with any other tool you employ.

My own adoption of Twitter as part of my training-teaching-learning-doing efforts (and as a useful tool in bringing successful community projects onsite and online to fruition) is a clear example of this process. I saw little use for Twitter as others were enthusiastically embracing it until the trusted colleague (mentioned in the preface to this book) who was a true Twitter aficionado spent a considerable amount of time trying to convince me that it could be a valuable tool for me. As we sat side by side over a two-day series of meetings, she occasionally and consistently would lean over to me and ask, "Did you know that, with Twitter, you could [fill in the blank]?" Each time she asked that question, I would patiently explain that whatever she was suggesting was something I was already doing through other means—until she finally suggested a way in which Twitter could fill an unmet need (in this case, helping me reach a large pool of prospective experts who could quickly help me find answers to research questions that were stumping me). The combination of a trusted source and a potential response to an unmet need led me to adopt Twitter fairly quickly at that point—but similar conversations with less-trusted (but no-less-enthusiastic) Twitter users over a two- or three-year period made the transition to becoming a Twitter user a delayed process for me.

As you consider incorporating Twitter, Facebook, and other social media tools into your own work, you'll find it well worth the time it takes to answer a couple of questions:

- Does the tool you are considering adopting fill an unmet need? If it doesn't, there's no point in immediately adopting it.
- Is the tool you are considering adopting in use by people with whom you want to collaborate in your effort to foster social change? If it isn't, there's no reason for you to go into a specific social media environment where your current and prospective collaborators don't go or aren't interested in going.

Change is often not easy, as I know from my own experience. I have, at times, even found it difficult to change where I go for my morning cup of coffee, the sandwich I inhale between meetings, or the glass of beer or wine or tea I relish at the end of a busy day of work or after an evening meal. Accepting the reality of that laughable level of opposition to some of the changes you might face, you would do well to choose social media tools that minimize the difficulties incurred by this change of tools. Save your energy for the substantial efforts you are going to make in pursuit of bringing positive, meaningful changes within your communities through the willing collaboration of your current and prospective partners.

HEALTHY SKEPTICISM AND FAKE NEWS: QUESTIONING YOUR SOURCES

There has always been plenty to make you skeptical about what you find online—both in terms of content and in terms of how you present yourself to others.

"Because of the nature of the Internet and social media, you have to be skeptical about who folks say they are," Maurice Coleman counsels. "Back in the Wild West days of the '90s and even before on old school BBS [bulletin board chat services], you could be talking to warmkitty96, thinking it was a lady in her twenties, and it is a guy in his sixties pretending to be a lady in her twenties online. You are talking to a screen name at first. You start engaging with words, and move on from there to deeper levels of communication. Just be aware is all."

Coleman and I cherish our library colleagues because they so effectively focus on helping us distinguish between reliable and unreliable sources of information in their collections as well as in online resources. We also cherish writers including Howard Rheingold and Donald Barclay, whose work helps us better understand the concept of digital literacy—being able to effectively select and use online resources to address our information and many other needs—and hone it so we can better achieve the goals we have for ourselves and the communities we serve.

Rheingold, in his book *Net Smart: How to Thrive Online*,[12] leads you through a series of discussions that better prepare you for some of the challenges you face in using social media and other elements of the Internet. His chapter on what he calls "crap detection" takes you to the heart of developing the skill to better differentiate between reliable sources and those that intentionally disseminate false information or openly exist as satirical sites, whose work is so effectively rooted in familiar situations as to be believable even though a quick examination of the sites' "About" pages reveals that the content is intentionally fictional. Examining those "About" pages, searching via Google and other search engines to gain background about the person or people identified as having produced the content on a website or in a social media account, and using fact-checking sites (e.g., Snopes[13]) offers a good start toward developing useful crap-detection skills.

Barclay, whose book *Fake News, Propaganda, and Plain Old Lies: How to Find Trustworthy Information in the Digital Age* [14] came to my attention through contact he made using a social media tool (LinkedIn), applies his skills as a librarian to endeavor to sift through information with an eye toward determining what is reliable and what is not. His chapters on "techniques that lower your information guard," "evaluating information sources" through "nine essential information questions everyone should ask," and "resources for evaluating information" are tremendously useful in helping you become a better sleuth in determining what is accurate and what is not, while helping you better understand and respond to techniques used by those who make you the target of false information.

NEXT STEPS

You have seen that the social aspect of social media platforms is often overlooked by those of us who use social media to broadcast ideas rather than engage in online conversations that sometimes extend into face-to-face encounters. Key elements of social media platforms include their inherent value as tools grounded in social interactions; the opportunities they offer and responsibilities they carry to foster engagement; and their blend of synchronous and asynchronous interactions that can occur across large geographic distances that previously would have served as barriers to quick and effective communication, planning, and action.

To gain a better understanding of how social media can produce positive opportunities and results for you and those you serve, please try either of the following exercises involving a step you are taking to promote a small- or large-scale change in a community with which you work:

- Create a post, on any of your social media accounts, that somehow encourages responses from those who see that post. Respond, within that social media platform, to any responses you receive to your initial post in an effort to create a positive, productive synchronous or asynchronous conversation designed to produce concrete results.

- Go to the ChangeTheWorld-Co community on Slack; initiate or join a discussion on that site in the channel designated for chapter 1; and respond to at least two of the responses your post inspires. (If you have not already joined that community, you can do so by contacting me directly at paul@paulsignorelli.com and including a brief—one-line—description of your interest in learning more about using social media to change the world.)

2

THE PROS AND CONS OF FACEBOOK

Facebook is the 800-pound gorilla of our current social media landscape. At its best, it can quickly and effectively put you in contact with colleagues all over the world. At its worst, it can leave you with the mistaken impression that you are reaching far more people than you are actually reaching, and can marginalize communities and individuals most in need of reaching others to achieve positive social change. In this chapter, you will see how others have used Facebook to foster small- and large-scale positive social change—at times in ways far beyond anything they could have imagined.

When Klaus Schwertner (Managing Director of Caritas in the Archdiocese of Vienna) posted a lovely photograph on Facebook to celebrate the first birth of the year in Vienna in January 2018, he could have had no idea that his sweetly intended routine action would attract thousands of comments and become the subject of an article in *The New York Times* within a few days.

There was nothing inherently alarming about that photograph; it showed a young husband and wife with their newborn baby girl shortly after the child was born. It was, for me, no different and no less heartwarming than any other "New Year's Baby" photo published in newspapers around the world during the past several decades or posted on Facebook or any other social media platform during the past several years.

This one, however, caused enough of a reaction to inspire Melissa Eddy to write the article that appeared in print and online editions of the newspaper on January 4—because the parents and child are Muslims, and the smiling mother in the photograph is wearing a pink scarf.[1] A version of the article in a print edition carried a headline capturing the initial shockingly brutal nature of many of the negative responses: "Vienna Welcomes 2018 Baby with Online Hate and Racism"; the online version that was also available as I was reading the print edition that morning included a more balanced, positive headline: "Vienna 'New Year's Baby' Greeted First with Hate, Then Hearts."

Those joining the online conversation extended the discussion beyond Facebook into Twitter, and the hashtag #GegenHassImNetz (AgainstHateOnTheNet) helped bring many of the online participants together, but the controversy didn't stop there. Schwertner's updates included a post expressing astonishment that someone at Facebook had taken down his original post about the birth—in which he playfully called for a "rain of flowers" to commemorate the birth. His follow-up post publicly asked Facebook Chairman/CEO Mark Zuckerberg for an explanation for the disappearance of the now-controversial post, and asked for help in restoring the post to Schwertner's Facebook timeline—an action that was taken later that day, to Schwertner's obvious delight.

"When you share something with the world, you're sharing it with a lot of people who don't think the way you do—who have different upbringings, values, and perspectives. If you believe in something, know that others believe in the opposite just as vehemently," Samantha Adams Becker, an independent consultant and President of SAB Creative & Consulting, notes. "There is still a lot of blind hate, and you have to separate the downright hateful reactions that have no basis. At the same time, the situations like the one you described . . . serve as an important reminder that though there has been a lot of social progress, we still have a long way to go. These kinds of incidents should incite more action towards positive change. Sadly, nothing brings people together like tragedy. It takes people's hope for change and inspires them to make it a reality, in service of helping people they care about who have been impacted."[2]

There are numerous elements worth examining here to better understand the power of incorporating Facebook into efforts to foster small- and large-scale positive changes through the use of social media. First and foremost is a recognition of how quickly even the most innocuous of posts on Facebook can become a central part of your responses to an issue you are interested in pursuing, e.g., the global effort to combat hate speech and bullying in public discourse by moving it into the context of #GegenHassImNetz. A second, nearly as important element is acceptance of the fact that what happens on Facebook doesn't stay on Facebook. My own awareness of the reaction to Schwertner's post didn't come via social media. It was a result of reading a copy of a print edition of *The New York Times* on January 4, 2018; feeling a mixture of amazement and horror as I read the language used against the parents and the child herself (solely because they were perceived to be different than those posting those hateful comments); using a mobile device to locate Schwertner's Facebook account and use Google Translate to examine the source material; discovering the #GegenHassIm-Netz hashtag (mentioned in the newspaper article) and subsequently exploring it to locate and read some of the positive comments posted on Twitter with that hashtag; and quickly deciding to take positive action by posting a link to the article—along with an expression of support for Schwertner, the parents, and the child—on my own Facebook account to draw my friends and colleagues into what had become a global conversation. (For more regarding online harassment, please see chapter 10.)

As noted in chapter 1, however, none of that takes full advantage of the potential power of social media if you and I ignore the social aspect of Facebook and other social media platforms. I decided to pursue the social side by sending a friend request to Schwertner as a way of reaching out to him to express support and determine whether he would be willing to discuss the situation for inclusion in this book. Although I never received a response (and, frankly, didn't expect one since he was at the center of a clearly unwanted maelstrom at that point), the fact that his story was accessible through Facebook and could be further disseminated through Facebook provided me with another example of how social media can provide an opportunity, at some level, to be part of a community that encourages someone—or something—in need of support.

Equally important is a third element built into any attempt to use Facebook or other social media channels to nurture social change: there is no guarantee that you are reaching those you are attempting to reach. You often have far less control and far less reach than is apparent. The removal of Schwertner's post reminds you that you cannot completely determine which of your online efforts remains accessible to those you want to reach, and the dissemination of Schwertner's subsequent messages hides a common problem encountered in posting on Facebook: the algorithms that determine who sees a post often result in those posts reaching far fewer members of an intended audience than expected—a topic more fully explored in the next section of this chapter.

Love it or hate it—and my colleagues and I often find ourselves having both reactions—there is no denying that Facebook is a potentially powerful tool that anyone interested in fostering positive social change has to understand at some level. As Tim O'Reilly notes in his book *WTF: What's the Future and Why It's Up to Us*, "Facebook is the defining company of the social era . . . it has challenged Google as the master of collective intelligence, uncovering an alternate routing system by which content is discovered and shared."[3]

That's a tool that cannot and will not be ignored.

INTRODUCTION TO FACEBOOK

The Executive Director of 18 Million Rising, Cayden Mak, gives a clear overview of Facebook:

> What I usually tell people is that there are two ways you can use Facebook. One is as a broadcast tool to get your message out there. It's cheaper in terms of time and effort. You probably don't want to spend that much time moderating a community there as a result, because it's less important what people think of you as a personality and more important that you reach people. But you'll probably spend more money on paid placement in the long-term, and if you have a budget for that, fine. [Facebook, for a fee, will boost your post to reach a larger audience.]
>
> The other way is this community-management route. You're going to have to develop norms for interaction, in order to build expectations among your audience. There's more of an investment in the frontend to get to that place, and this is treating Facebook less as a broadcast medium than a semipublic forum that allows people to weigh in on issues. I personally prefer this because then it's more likely that those people's friends will see your stuff organically. It also

makes more sense from an organizing perspective, I think. Thinking about how to create those norms is frontloading the work a bit, and empowering your team to make decisions in the moment is critical. Also, cultivating mindfulness—which is becoming such a meaningless buzzword—but honestly, getting to the point where you can take a step back from someone's incendiary words and ask, "Do I think this person is engaging in good faith?" If so, how can we avoid confrontations that will produce bad feelings, and, instead, direct the energy into a learning opportunity? Conflict is inevitable. It's how you deal with it that separates the good organizers from the merely average.[4]

Because there are so many first-rate guides available in print and online and because Facebook and other social media tools evolve quickly and unpredictably, I'm going to offer only the most cursory of introductions to how Facebook works, has already evolved, and has drawn abundant praise as well as ample criticism. For those in search of detailed introductions to a variety of topics related to Facebook and how it can be used for general purposes, I highly recommend the continually updated Wikipedia article on Facebook[5]—particularly the sections on "User profile/personal timeline," "News Feed," "Privacy," "Criticisms and controversies," and "Political Impact" because they offer some finely nuanced discussions of the ever-changing state of the Facebook universe—and the latest edition of *Facebook for Dummies*[6] for its user-friendly, step-by-step approach to the subject. The Facebook online Help Center[7] is also obviously a good resource for up-to-date information about how to set up and manage your Facebook account.

A good starting point is to recognize what Facebook is and what it isn't: "I think . . . it's a platform that's ultimately designed to keep you on the feed as long as possible, while maximizing revenue through ad views," 18 Million Rising Social Media Manager Tony Choi suggests. "It could be a powerful tool connecting us in ways unimaginable, but oftentimes, it's just us gawking at one another."[8]

It is, furthermore, part of the Internet "surveillance capitalism" landscape described in great detail by Shoshana Zuboff in *The Age of Surveillance Capitalism: The Fight for a Human Future at the New Frontier of Power*.[9] Referring to Facebook's "self-authorizing practice of behavior modification at scale,"[10] Zuboff meticulously reviews how Facebook, without users' knowledge or consent, has engaged in experiments to determine how they would respond to manipulation of information contained in or excluded from their Facebook news feeds. The results, along with numerous other situations she documents, lead her to suggest that there is need to "reestablish our bearings" in terms of what we do and do not accept from those providing us with services online: "I have asked for a rebirth of astonishment and outrage," she writes.[11]

Facebook, clearly, is one of the premier, most heavily used social media tools at the time of this writing.[12] It provides an online global meeting place where users themselves—within the guidelines Facebook itself creates and updates in response to the ever-changing social media environment—determine how serious or frivolous that platform will be; through your own posts and choices regarding what you read and to which items you respond, you have a hand in shaping your experience on that platform. It offers you ways (through the use of privacy settings) to at least partially control what you see and who sees the items you post on your account's timeline (the display of all your posts)—but there are plenty of exceptions, so I strongly advise you to follow a very simple practice: if there's something you don't want everyone in the world to see, don't post it. An earlier incarnation of Facebook included direct-messaging capabilities as part of the overall platform, but the messaging tool now exists as a stand-alone app.

"Facebook allows you to set up 'groups' to post to," FutureWe Founder Jonathan Nalder counsels. "This lets you send certain messages to only certain people. So, for me, I have 300 close friends and family I can limit personal posts to—and then could also set up a group just for educators, just for Australians, etc.—so I'd encourage people to make a group to test out posts and learn about posting in that smaller, safer way."[13]

Facebook is clearly not a guaranteed way to reach everyone with whom you want to interact. The algorithms that Facebook creates and uses determine which of your posts are seen by parts of your overall community of Facebook "friends."[14] (Those friends are the people who have accepted your invitation to communicate via Facebook and who have access to your posts because you have not screened them out through the use of the privacy settings you can and should regularly review to be sure they reflect your own current preferences.) The result of the use of those algorithms is that some of your posts may be seen by a large percentage of your Facebook friends (changes in your Facebook profile picture tend to reach and draw responses from a large percentage) while others (particularly posts unaccompanied by a picture or a video) may be seen by and draw reactions from almost none of them. There are numerous reasons why this is true; one of the most important is that Facebook employees are trying to keep all of us from being completely overwhelmed by a flood of information through which we would be completely incapable of sifting in our Facebook news feed (the list of items that appear for us to view and respond to). A change made by Facebook in January 2018 further changes the dynamic of what appears in your news feed by promoting content from people you know rather than from media outlets.[15]

You can increase the frequency with which a friend's posts appear in your own news feed (and, therefore, become quickly visible to you when you view your account) by using the News Feed Preferences settings in your account. Viewing your Facebook friends' accounts and posts regularly and reacting to them with comments or something as simple as a "like" are another way to increase the likelihood that at least some of their posts will appear in your news feed.

One simple example of how this works comes from my own activities in using Facebook while writing this book. As I identified people and organizations that appeared to be good resources, I started following their accounts and actively adding them to my group of Facebook friends. Their posts immediately began appearing in my news feed with some regularity, and I also began receiving Facebook recommendations for other organizations and individuals who might be—and often proved to be—of interest to me as I explored a variety of positive examples of how Facebook served as a useful tool for those fostering positive change in small as well as large onsite and online communities.

This provides another reminder of how various social media tools, used in combination, provide a rich environment for developing the contacts and relationships to foster positive change. As I became more familiar with some of the people quoted in this book, I routinely looked to see what they were doing on Twitter, LinkedIn, and other platforms; this helped me decide which platforms provided the most useful forms of access to those individuals.

"You may be limiting your audience of supporters if you only use Facebook to organize for social justice. It should be a well-used engagement tool, but not the only tool," Harford County Public Library Tech Trainer Maurice Coleman counsels. [16]

———༄༄༄———

On Algorithms and Marginalization
Cayden Mak

I think the big challenges for people looking to build real community engagement on Facebook are both procedural—such as the algorithms that determine what stories are delivered to people's news feeds—and human—their shitty content filtering, for instance. On the procedural side, there's just not a lot of transparency and control. It's in Facebook's interest to keep it that way, and in order to make money on their business, they want to encourage organizations and companies to utilize paid placement of stories in order to reach users of all stripes. That's just not helpful for small or grassroots groups who don't have an advertising budget.

On the more human side, Facebook continually fails more marginalized communities in the way it filters content, and there's a whole lot of layers to this, from bad or completely absent standards-setting—we've seen a lot of *post hoc* standards being put in place thanks to advocacy from a coalition we participate in along with the Center for Media Justice and *Daily Kos* and Color of Change—to a huge reliance on either machine learning that is inherently biased or, perhaps worse than that, highly traumatized, low-paid pieceworkers with no context for certain kinds of language. That's why you see so many stories that, for instance, critique certain uses of racial slurs being censored even if they are specifically advocating against their use. There just isn't a good way to do this work at scale, and I don't think Facebook is trying very hard to be honest.

———༄༄༄———

As a learning facilitator, I have often looked for ways to incorporate Facebook and other social media tools into my efforts to foster the much smaller, far-less-dramatic levels of positive change that are inherent in effective learning endeavors. In onsite courses and workshops, as well as in online courses that are primarily asynchronous, I continually seek ways to use social media to create venues for live, in-the-moment learning opportunities; this also works well in asynchronous learning opportunities, e.g., for learners who participate, after the fact, in webinars by listening/viewing them through online archives. Experiments have ranged from the use of Facebook groups to conduct live online office hours through typed chat (with chat transcripts that can later be shared with those unable to attend the live sessions) to the use of Facebook groups to foster entire long-term communities of interest that continue to learn together long after a course has formally ended. There is no reason why you can't be using Facebook community pages or Facebook groups, as Jonathan Nalder mentioned in the previous section of this chapter, to conduct your own conversations, planning efforts, and other collaborations that lead you and members of your communities to use the groups in this way—as long as you or someone else in a group is comfortable with and well-versed in the art of facilitating online conversations.

Samantha Adams Becker, during her time with the NMC (New Media Consortium), took Facebook-as-a-learning-platform to new heights—in ways that might serve any activist with a need to train others who are part of efforts to promote social change through the use of social media tools. Designing and facilitating "Applications of Social Media for STEMx Teaching"—the first course to ever be offered entirely on Facebook—Becker saw Facebook as the right tool for the right learning opportunity; her online classroom was a Facebook community page similar to those I have experienced as part of—rather than being at the center of—other online learning opportunities. Becker recalls the process of creating this course:

> The logic was that the message must fit the medium, and the subject matter of the course revolved around teaching education professionals how to use social media for teaching and learning. Using Facebook for the course was intended to get people to learn by doing—by experiencing it firsthand. When designing the course, it was important to expose learners to the very same features I wanted them to be able to take advantage of in their own environments.
>
> A key characteristic of all social media is the asynchronous factor: users should be able to connect and learn whenever they want, from wherever they want. Education opportunities are following suit. Posting videos and articles that people could access in a self-paced manner made sense in this dynamic, while any posts/announcements

from me should have comments enabled so learners could start spin-off discussions.

Another attractive quality about Facebook is that the appeal is strikingly simple—consuming and sharing. People depend on it for news/updates about other people—and organizations—and as a way to let their network know what is going on in their lives. The course was inspired by this simplicity. It showcased resources for better understanding social media, tools and ideas for integrating it into teaching and learning, and provided participants with a community of education professionals to share their experiences at any given time—to ask questions, to push each other further. Plus, since Facebook is social by nature, it made keeping in touch beyond the course seamless. [17]

Incorporating Facebook into outreach efforts is continuing to grow as those familiar with Facebook dream of new ways to incorporate it into their work. Take, for instance, Topeka and Shawnee County Public Library Digital Services Director David Lee King:

We haven't done this yet, but we want to start holding a series of in-person community events that focus around current topics. We'd probably start with a more innocuous one, but then maybe move towards more hot topics like civil rights issues, or bridging those political divides that everyone is seeing.

Social media would definitely play a role in that. Starting with the event invitations and reminders, to monitoring and sharing people's thoughts and responses during and after the event.

Could be fun, could be useful, could be messy. Probably all of those things. . . . We've experimented with Facebook Live [video streaming]; it would be pretty easy to livestream the event to get more conversation going, especially in the Topeka area. We could also share hashtags to get people who couldn't attend to follow and share their thoughts. [18]

━◢◯◯◣━

Levels of Engagement through Facebook

The use of Facebook in planning and implementing the initial Women's March in January 2017 "provided grassroots authenticity, and that it wasn't just [comprised of] the Hillary Clinton campaign remnants who were bitter about the election loss," Tony Choi recalls in his capacity as one of the original organizers of the marches.

> The energy on social media showed that it was a diverse coalition that showed immigrant rights, racial justice, and all these other issues were women's rights. It also gave the March a platform that it defined by itself, whereas, with traditional media, it would have had to work to fit into a narrative.
>
> We were anticipating that it would be big, but definitely not to [that large a] scale. When we heard the number [was] in the hundreds of thousands, it didn't feel real. But what struck me were certain moments. When we saw pictures of women in pink hats marching in Boise in the snow, that's when it hit me as real. I bawled. It felt real when I was at Target, picking up a printer the night before, and they announced that they were out of poster paper. I hugged the Target employee who helped me, and I cried so much. And we're still feeling the impacts today. Many of the women who won seats in the Virginia House of Delegates were inspired by the march to run. We'll continue to see impacts for sure.[19]

—◦◦◦—

Facebook was also one of many tools used to create awareness of and support for a major community collaborative project in San Francisco from January 2010 through December 2013: the creation of San Francisco's Hidden Garden Steps,[20] which features the second of what are now six large-scale ceramic-tiled staircases in residential neighborhoods. The Hidden Garden Steps, with its mosaic and volunteer-maintained public gardens on the west side of the city, has become a place where neighbors, instead of avoiding the site because of graffiti-filled walls and a garbage-strewn hillside, now meet, talk, and dream of even bigger things alongside visitors from all over the world. The project, very much inspired by completion of a similar project four blocks away from the second set of concrete steps, actually began with an unanticipated meeting between two of us in our neighborhood and Colette Crutcher, who with Aileen Barr designed and fabricated the 163-step mosaic for the original (16th Avenue Tiled Steps) ceramic-tiled staircase completed in August 2005.[21] The Hidden Garden Steps organizing committee, formed shortly after that first conversation with Crutcher, was supported by dozens of volunteers who worked with City-County of San Francisco representatives; neighbors; local business owners; representatives of nonprofit organizations; and just about anyone else who expressed the slightest bit of interest in the project. The volunteer-managed Facebook page[22] became one of several online resources for posts—often featuring a combination of short, playfully written project updates, colorful photographs, videos, and, most importantly, invitations to join the Steps community. This helped create the massive levels of support needed to bring the $467,000 project to fruition. The Facebook page slowly and steadily grew from having a handful of followers in 2013 to having over 1,100 in January 2020, and having attracted more than 6,700 check-ins from visitors. It remains active as an online Oldenburgian third place[23] (a place that, because people routinely meet there socially, contributes to the sense and strength of a community), offering everything from reports about how the mosaic and gardens continue to attract visitors to information about other projects and activities of interest to those who supported and continue to support the project. It also remains ready to serve as a resource to the next group interested in creating a similar project anywhere in the world.

The levels of conversation and positive action proposed by David Lee King and seen through the Hidden Garden Steps and many other projects are also evident in Nalder's FutureWe project to prepare learners for a world in which substantial numbers of jobs are going to evolve radically or simply disappear during the next couple of decades and be replaced by opportunities that are not yet fully apparent.[24]

"One of the big goals of the FutureWe community is to enable the kinds of conversations that need to get started if we are to be even partly prepared for a post-work era," Nalder notes. "I have one-on-one chats and meet with small groups all the time, but that's hugely complemented by (a) reaching thousands of people via Facebook, etc., and (b) seeing them share the conversation onto their networks. The fact that this is all done in micro-moments via the super-efficient interface of Facebook—where it's just tapping and only takes a few seconds—means that even if it's not as deep as a face-to-face or longer chat, the amplified possibilities are hugely helpful."[25]

The positive results to be gained through effective use of Facebook in promoting positive social change are apparent: "Because of the connectivity of Facebook, you can either publicly engage someone on an issue or send them a private message to back-channel books or articles or engage in social change organizing," Maurice Coleman notes. "You can post pretty innocuous things publicly, but can have a private presence in a closed group or via [Facebook] Messenger that is fiery or change-making without having to readily acknowledge it publicly. You can play the role of connector of folks on Facebook by introducing folks who have things in common with each other—[the connection] mostly being you."[26]

Cayden Mak has also seen magnificent results from efforts to use Facebook in converting potential supporters into enthusiastic participants in the movement-building process:

> First and foremost, Facebook is a huge powerhouse for conversions, i.e., people seeing an available campaign and taking action for the first time. We get the most growth on campaigns we run from good Facebook content, and in order to reach those people, you need to be consistent and thoughtful about sharing stuff on your page.
>
> Because of the mysterious way the Facebook news feed algorithm gets tweaked, sometimes what works changes. But overall, over time, we've seen the most new members come in through Facebook than [through] any other platform. People are much more likely to click a link they see on Facebook as opposed to Twitter—one of the advantages of the platform is that it's designed to send people out into the broader Internet—although less and less lately—as opposed to Twitter, where the entire platform is meant to be an all-inclusive environment. It's the big reason we can't ditch it.
>
> It also seems to be a place where people are a little more willing to sit and think about something than on Twitter, where things devolve into shouting matches much more quickly. With a little personal touch, Facebook turns into a platform where people can, and do, ask somewhat more complex questions about topics we work with. Careful community management/stewardship helps build a culture of inquiry on a page, and that's something that we invest heavily in. Whether it's judicious banning or gentle pushing back on people who have opinions that are a little derisive, the time spent there makes a difference.[27]

The conversations initiated or continued on Facebook can also be useful to a certain extent in fundraising to change the world (a topic more fully explored in chapter 9 of this book). EveryLibrary Political Director Patrick Sweeney confirms this:

> The thing to remember is that it's a really long process. Social media ads that ask for donations just don't work. You can't run an ad that says "give us $10" and expect to get back more than you spend. It either doesn't work, or I don't know how to write those ads in a way that draws in donations. So, about one-half to three-fourths of our spending is just about communicating with our audience about who we are and what we do and why libraries are important. We also use it to open dialogues with audiences of people so it's not a one-sided conversation. The other one-half to one-fourth is on direct action, such as signing petitions, joining coalitions, etc. And it's those actions that yield our donations . . .
>
> We are using Facebook to identify volunteers and find the kinds of people who want to be engaged at a much deeper level. So, we have volunteer sign-up forms and everything. We also organize volunteer days and other events for volunteers to get involved, but we've gotten mixed results with that. Still, the only people [who] showed up were people who had more personal relationships to us beyond just Facebook ads or posts or whatever.[28]

Pro Tips: Facebook

"Staying relevant to the subject is important. Sharing personal stories is an important way to emotionally resonate with people around the cause you support, but it does make you vulnerable simply by your story going viral. It's a balancing act of generating exposure for your social change cause with exposure for yourself as a person."—Samantha Adams Becker, who uses Facebook to foster change through learning

"Find [your] own fearless voice and stick to it. And build community with people who share your voice."—Tony Choi, who has used Facebook through his work with 18 Million Rising

"If you are introducing two people to each other, tell them individually that you think A should know B and why and vice versa via individual messages. Then let them make a connection, if they choose. . . . Model appropriate to the audience behavior at all times."—Maurice Coleman, who uses Facebook to promote positive change through training-teaching-learning

"First and foremost, trust people. I know it's hard online, but the majority of people *do* arrive with good intentions. They want to learn. They want to interact. It's pretty obvious, I think, who is acting in bad faith. The other thing is not to get into a back-and-forth with that bad-faith actor . . . it's your space and you have the right to deal with them judiciously. I think that when you do that, other people see that as a signal that their good-faith participation is welcome and, in fact, protected. It also saves you the time, energy, and mental anguish of talking to some asshole who sets up straw men just to make you look like a jerk."—Cayden Mak, who uses Facebook through his work with 18 Million Rising

"I . . . have found that honest participation—not just a spontaneous ban from a moderator—is the best way to manage community online. When the people who come back time and time again see you speaking and behaving in a consistent manner, regardless of whether it's breaking up fights or offering insight into something that you shared, they get to feel like they know you. Learn by doing and chatting with other people you know on there, and by finding key people in your area who are already sharing successfully and watch and learn from them."—Jonathan Nalder, who uses Facebook to promote change through communities of learning

"Accept change. . . . Everything [every social media platform] changes, nothing stays the same. . . . People get very attached to certain platforms and modes of communication. When these start to change, people don't like to change with them."—Elizabeth Myers, who uses Facebook to support positive change within the community she serves

—————

Facebook has also been a useful tool on some of EveryLibrary's campaigns, Sweeney notes.

> We used Facebook to drive our petition to fight against the closure of libraries in Mary Esther, Florida. The town board was going to close the library so they could hire another sheriff, and the Sheriff's

Department was pushing really hard for them to do it. It meant more money for police, and the complete loss of the library.

So, we worked with the folks on the ground in Mary Esther to put a petition together. We used our large network on Facebook and our email to make this a national issue. Small-time local politicians often hate it when their decisions become negative national news. So, we ran a ton of dark ads in Mary Esther and the surrounding area as well as national organic ads, and they got their email blown up by the response. Having that large network on Facebook who are already familiarized with our work and the threats to libraries that already existed meant that people were prepped and ready to take action like sending emails to the town council.[29]

WHEN TO RETREAT

The levels of engagement possible through Facebook and other social media platforms bring an obvious challenge with them: information overload, also known as "when to turn it off." We are in an environment where Ray Oldenburg's three places in our lives—home, work, and play[30]—are blending together inextricably onsite and online. Recognizing how to maintain a balance that feels healthy and productive for yourself and those you serve through your efforts is increasingly challenging. Markham Public Library Community Librarian Elizabeth Myers speaks to this balancing act:

> The whole idea [is] that too much of a good thing—friends, family, connection—can be emotionally draining. It's really the best things in life that you shouldn't overindulge in; professionally, it could be construed as "don't overshare, don't undershare, just Goldilocks it."
> . . .
> The lines [between our work and personal lives] have definitely blurred. I try to create my own boundaries, but it's still ever-present—the personal and professional social connections—in my life both at work and at home. . . . You want to create social change, and you're passionate, so the reaction is to sometimes share more in the hope that if you just get the information out there and tell more people and shout it from the mountaintops, the change will happen. That's not how the world works, though.

The people—professionally and personally, double p's—who incessantly share and post and throw themselves out there—I'm speaking specifically about Facebook here—are the people you want to avoid. Not that you don't agree with what they're saying, or that you wouldn't be interested in engaging otherwise, but the platform doesn't really work very well with word vomit.[31]

NEXT STEPS

To gain a better understanding of how the use of Facebook can produce positive opportunities and results for you and those you serve, please try either of the following exercises involving a step you are taking to promote a small- or large-scale change in a community with which you work:

- Create a post on Facebook and somehow encourage responses from those who see that post; respond, within Facebook, to any responses you receive to your initial post.
- Go to the ChangeTheWorld-Co community on Slack; initiate or join a discussion on that site in the channel designated for chapter 2; and respond to at least two of the responses your post inspires. (If you have not already joined that community, you can do so by contacting me directly at paul@paulsignorelli.com and including a brief—one-line—description of your interest in learning more about using social media to change the world.)

3

TWITTER—SMALL MESSAGES WITH LARGE RESULTS

Twitter is an extremely popular social media platform that encourages brevity through its 280-character-per-post limit. It can connect you to colleagues and supporters globally at a variety of levels, allowing you to view content without responding or, at the opposite end of the spectrum of levels of engagement, conduct in-the-moment conversations through your tweets. In this chapter, you will see how the use of carefully chosen keywords (hashtags), sessions involving conversation-by-Twitter, and backchannels (online conversations, via Twitter, that extend the reach of onsite and online activities) can be an important part of your overall effort to foster positive change.

If you want to viscerally understand the power of Twitter, think of the global impact two small words ("me too") and their translations into other languages have had. Capturing an enormous emotionally nuanced message (we all know someone affected by sexual harassment and/or assault, so what are we going to do about it?), those two words have been repeated countless times to inspire positive action by men and women using Twitter and other social media platforms. Those two words were used by actress Alyssa Milano in a tweet on October 15, 2017: "Suggested by a friend: 'If all the women who have been sexually harassed or assaulted wrote "Me too" as a status, we might give people a sense of the magnitude of the problem.'"[1] Milano quickly achieved her goal of increasing awareness regarding sexual harassment and assault: the hashtag draws attention to the often dramatically different reactions people have to the allegations and reality of sexual harassment at local, regional, national, and international levels. I was among those made even more painfully aware of the prevalence of sexual harassment and assault by this hashtag. It has drawn me—and many friends, acquaintances, and colleagues—into efforts to shine a spotlight on it and combat it at whatever level we can—via social media, through face-to-face conversations, and through support for actions that can decrease the presence of harassment and assault whenever we see opportunities to do so.

Let me be clear about the role Twitter and other social media platforms played in what has, through the use of the #MeToo hashtag, become another highly visible and extended global conversation (and sometimes bitter argument) about sexual harassment and sexual abuse. The conversation did not start with the breaking of a significant news story on Twitter, nor did the hashtag #MeToo become a widely recognized unifying call to action the same day it was created. (The hashtag was first used by social activist Tarana Burke in 2006.[2]) Stories about sexual harassment and abuse in a variety of settings—including workplaces, schools and universities, and religious organizations—have been published and discussed for several decades by those who accept the veracity of the allegations and want to make positive changes, as well as by those who deny the allegations and object to what they see as exaggerations or outright falsehoods. Attitudes and disagreements about sexual harassment and sexual abuse were clearly on display during the 2016 presidential campaign in the United States when a recording capturing Donald Trump boasting, in 2005, of his ability to harass and assault women was widely disseminated through traditional and social media outlets.[3]

The #MeToo conversation expanded rapidly after articles published in *The New York Times* (October 5, 2017[4]) and *The New Yorker* (October 10, 2017[5]) documented gut-wrenching allegations that Miramax entertainment company and The Weinstein Company co-founder Harvey Weinstein had engaged in sexual harassment and sexual abuse involving dozens of women in the film industry for at least two decades. Reading the first lengthy and well-documented story in *The New York Times* that October morning left me disgusted and heartsick; I found it difficult to even finish reading the article as I thought about this latest set of allegations showing how someone in a position of power could take advantage of people perceived to have less—or no—voice than those who were making their lives miserable.

———◦◦◦———

On Hashtags

Hashtags, represented by what previously was known as a pound, number, or hash sign (#), are a user- rather than Twitter-initiated innovation—a reminder that much of what happens in the development of social media tools grows out of user as well as company innovations. They were born in 2007 when Chris Messina, who describes himself online with the terms "product guy, inventor of the hashtag, ex-Uber, ex-Google, and friend to startups,"[6] decided to use it as a way to organize content on Twitter and refer to it as a hashtag.[7]

The concept is simple: by beginning a word or uninterrupted group of words (e.g., #OccupyWallStreet) with the pound sign, users become content-organizers within Twitter by creating a way for others to find information on a commonly shared topic of interest. Other online tools—including Tweetdeck and Hootsuite—allow users to easily aggregate content by hashtags. This means you can see an entire stream of content from tweeters all over the world in a single column of seemingly infinite text, images, and links; retweet (share) that content so it stands a better chance of being noticed by those who follow you on Twitter; and engage in conversations both in immediate moments of time as well as the extended moments of time described in chapter 1. And although there has been plenty of discussion recently as to whether hashtags are dying, the most proficient social media users I know still contend what I believe: they are effective tools for helping others find the content you are providing via social media.[8]

Cara McGoogan, writing in *The Telegraph* on the tenth anniversary of the creation of the hashtag, notes that as of August 2017, "(a)round 125 million hashtags are shared by Twitter's 328 million users every day. The popular icon has since been picked up by other networks, including Instagram, Tumblr, and Facebook."[9]

The use of hashtags continues to grow in numerous ways that bring members of communities of interest together virtually. Attendees at conferences can draw offsite participants into their discussions by establishing and publicizing standard hashtags for anyone interested in conversations via Twitter. Members of learning communities can communicate globally through synchronous online discussions known as tweet chats. (Please see the "Engagement through Tweet Chats" section in this chapter for more information.) Activists can and do use hashtags to initiate tweet chats and other online uses of Twitter to mobilize, share resources, plan, and implement plans of action.

———◦◦◦———

Absorbing the numerous follow-up reports about Weinstein and many others became even more emotionally challenging when women—lots of women, far beyond the boundaries of the entertainment industry scandals documented in *The New York Times* and *The New Yorker*—began using #MeToo to acknowledge themselves as recipients of unwanted sexual attention by friends, acquaintances, employers, workplace colleagues, or complete strangers. I was absolutely stunned by the large number of women I knew who eloquently joined the conversation through short #MeToo posts. And that's one of the many ways in which the power of Twitter and other social media tools becomes apparent: what at one time would have been stories about someone else continually become stories about those I know and love and care for. Twitter and other social media platforms provide a way for voices that might otherwise not have been heard to be heard in ways that inspire people to work together to actively promote the changes they want to see to create the world of their dreams. What might at one time have been stories told within small, isolated groups of people or discussed in local communities became stories shared globally—and very quickly.

"The #MeToo movement is an obvious, but powerful, one [an example of Twitter used to effectively promote social change]," Samantha Adams Becker, the independent consultant and President of SAB Creative & Consulting, observes. "Suddenly, people who were scared to share something deeply personal were empowered to tell their stories because other people were doing it. I don't think that movement could have spread as rapidly on any other platform because of [the] continuous-conversation factor. There's Snapchat, Instagram, and new social platforms emerging all the time, but Twitter has remained loyal to the idea of words. And in spite of the growth of videos and infographics, etc. Words. Are. Still. *Powerful* currency."[10]

Shining a social media spotlight on those situations you want to change is often seen as positive even in the worst of situations; it is, therefore, well worth noting that the same shining spotlight, used with less-than-honorable intentions, can cause tremendous grief for those unfairly targeted—a theme more fully explored in chapter 10. Using Twitter and other social media platforms carries tremendous responsibility—a responsibility that often is inadvertently or intentionally overlooked by users. As you consider incorporating—or further incorporating—Twitter into your social media tool kit, you would do well to follow advice frequently given throughout this book: think before you post. If you are in doubt as to whether your tweet meets the highest, most positive ethical standards to which you subscribe, don't post. Tweets and other posts can wait; once they are out there, they are impossible to undo.

There is obviously plenty to be done with Twitter to positively change your world; it begins with using it to give voice to those—you and many others—whose voices are not often enough clearly heard. You already have examples from some of the hashtags mentioned at the beginning of chapter 1 (e.g., #ArabSpring, #BlackLivesMatter, #ClimateStrike/#FridaysForFuture, #DACA, #Ferguson, #MAGA/MakeAmericaGreatAgain, #MarchForOurLives/#NeverAgain, #OccupyWallStreet, and #ParisAccord) of the impact a well-designed and well-used hashtag can have. Whether you agree or disagree with the goals implicit in the movements represented by those hashtags, you can easily recognize that their effective use is part of contemporary social and political discourse—a resource not to be ignored by anyone involved in activism.

INTRODUCTION TO TWITTER

Twitter, referred to at times as a micro-blogging resource as well as a social networking tool and an online news service, was initially envisioned by its creators (in 2006) as a way for small groups of individuals to communicate online through "a short burst of inconsequential information"; it quickly developed into something far beyond its creators' wildest dreams by becoming a global social networking tool.[11]

As commonly happens within social media platforms, its format continues to evolve. It originally had a limit of 140 characters per tweet;

that limit was doubled in November 2017.[12] It has evolved from a text-based service into one that includes images and provides a tool for creating and posting very short videos.

Twitter's rapid growth and evolution has been spectacular, growing from 400,000 tweets posted by users during the first three months of 2007 to approximately 65 million per day by June 2010[13] and an average of more than 500 million per day when I was updating data for this chapter in January 2020.[14]

"Twitter is my town crier and headline maker," Harford County Public Library Tech Trainer Maurice Coleman admits. "Brief stuff, links, etc. When it was 140 characters, you really had to self-edit and pull a crucible. With 280, more characters equals more gasbaggery."[15]

"Even early on, it allowed me to go far beyond being just one local teacher to where I could access a whole globe's worth of ideas to help me grow—and also to build a network where I could be heard and even share inspiration in the first place," FutureWe Founder Jonathan Nalder recalls.[16]

It is also a service and a tool that provides overwhelming amounts of content that engender even more content through repeated posts and retweeting (the act of forwarding someone else's tweet through your own account so the information reaches your friends/followers who may not have seen the original post). "Twitter is everything, as it happens. It's more like a huge river of content that goes by as it happens," Topeka and Shawnee County Public Library Digital Services Director David Lee King points out. "If you want to make sure all your Twitter followers see something, you have to post multiple times, at different times of the day. So, it's really good for in-the-moment conversations, but not as good at the 'I want to make sure everyone sees this' type of communication."[17]

Not surprisingly, developing a consistent, effective presence and set of goals on Twitter and other social media platforms takes a lot of work, 18 Million Rising Executive Director Cayden Mak says:

> Being a person or entity that people feel comfortable interacting with beyond breaking news requires a lot of time and energy—individual replies, a consistency in tone and analysis, and participating in lots of real-time events. We gain lots of followers when we do stuff like live-tweet awards ceremonies like the Oscars with snark, humor, and perspective. That's how we get people in the door. Then, when

it's back to the everyday grind, those people learn about the issues we're working on, and about people and organizations we are in community with. It's very powerful in that way, but it requires both the skill to make it work and the time to make good on the commitment.

There is more than one way to use a tool like Twitter. You need to decide, in the context of your campaign, how you're going to do that. Sometimes the most obvious way—as another channel to broadcast your work—isn't the most fruitful, especially knowing what we know about how people using Twitter are less likely to click and leave the Twitter environment. So, [you need to ask] what can you do to get people *in* that environment to do something that strengthens your work?[18]

A corollary to the theme of creating an online persona is the theme of controlling whose posts you see. Some, as Syracuse University Associate Professor of Practice Jill Hurst-Wahl notes, prefer Twitter to Facebook because of their sense that they can more easily and effectively control what comes through their online feeds:

Facebook aims for two-way communications with people you are "friends" with, but they may not be close friends, and perhaps you don't want to see their stuff. I much prefer the Twitter model, where I can follow someone who doesn't need to follow me back.

In Facebook, there is a mutual agreement that when you accept my friends request, we will follow each other and see each other's posts [although it is possible to surreptitiously block posts from friends from appearing in your Facebook feed]. Yes, I can unfollow you, but that weeding of the friends list in Facebook is not easy. . . . In Twitter, I can more easily follow people and place them into lists. Then it is up to me to check those lists—I use Hootsuite. You do not have to follow me back. So, tons of people follow me, but I don't follow them back. They see my stuff, but I don't see their stuff. And people have built tools that help me weed my Twitter followers. Those tools can be clunky, because of Twitter's API, but at least they exist and I can use them.[19]

———◦/◦/◦———

On Tweeting, Walking, and Building Community

It began with a response, via Twitter, to a tweet initiated through the Markham Public Library (Toronto, Canada), Community Librarian Elizabeth Myers recalls. It led to a seventy-person neighborhood walk, in October 2017, to "emphasize the experiences of Islamic Canadians," with the goal of bringing neighbors together through a shared sense of connection though story in a city "undergoing . . . a hard cultural shift."

Markham, Myers explains, was "a rural agricultural community with a large base of Mennonite and German farmers" more than half a century ago; since then, it has become "home to one of the largest diasporas of Chinese people outside of China"—a place where nearly sixty percent of the residents do not speak English in their homes. It is also a city with "wide roads, big houses, and lots of construction and development"—a place where people drive rather than walk, and where "pedestrians can sometimes appear to be invisible."

> This is where I come in, and the work that I do comes in. . . . What does everyone want their community to be? Walkable. They don't want to *have* to drive. They want the versatility and the options to walk. They want a connected, vibrant, safe, walkable community. The question my community partner and I asked then, was: How does a community become walkable unless people start walking?
>
> The response that we got from the community was indicative of the desire to connect with their community, to connect with their neighbors. That's the whole idea behind social media, isn't it? . . . Connection. Networks. What's a neighborhood? Who are your neighbors? That's part of your personal network. By actively engaging with your community and taking action, you are creating change. That is evident in the response on social media and to the event itself. Seventy people came out on a cloudy, rainy, October morning to go for a walk in a community that doesn't walk.
>
> Our goal of facilitating this connection and living action to develop community was to engage people's natural urge to connect with others by telling stories. Stories are where you find common ground—where even the most different of people can find a spark of connection. . . .
>
> Leading up to the event and during the event, there was a social media presence. Afterwards, there were extended interactions on

social media—like another library connecting their experiences with ours—and also developing connections with local educators and with families, mothers, and fathers who interacted with the library on social media. The relationship has continued to grow and connect in different ways.[20]

———⌇⌇⌇———

Twitter provides an interesting extension of a theme initially explored in chapter 1—the idea that a "moment" of time can be much different than the traditional measurement reflected by simply glancing at a clock to determine how much time has passed. "Twitter enables positive social changes by transcending the necessity of a specific time and place," Samantha Adams Becker agrees. "A conversation about climate change, for example, may begin between two people. Another person sees the tweet and then joins. And then another. And then another. [This process is more fully explored in chapter 11 through a review of #ClimateStrike/#FridaysForFuture activist Greta Thunberg's activities.] The people are geographically dispersed and may not be using Twitter at the exact same time but, because Twitter sparks continuous conversation, people can join on their own time whenever they have something to contribute. And the asynchronous nature of it doesn't detract from the subject matter or substance of it. In fact, pausing to think deeply about something before joining in *is* an important part of change."[21]

While you can learn a lot by simply observing how those you admire use Twitter, you don't have to admire a group or organization's political views to admire its effectiveness, Coleman notes. He cited the #MAGA [MakeAmericaGreatAgain] movement as one he admires for its "sheer numbers" and "news-spreading" abilities.[22]

LEVELS OF ENGAGEMENT THROUGH TWITTER

Some, including Becker, find tremendous levels of engagement through Twitter:

I think Twitter—more so than any other social media platform—allows for continuous conversation. If one of your Facebook friends made 10 posts per day, you might find that a bit excessive. However, you may find it completely acceptable that a friend tweets 10 times in a day. That reaction alone points to Twitter as a much more embraced conversation/sharing platform. Not only can a discussion continue between multiple users, but you can continue your own conversation. . . . Perhaps most essentially, a conversation you may have started in person can continue on Twitter. This seems to be very popular at conferences where you may have a brief encounter with a person who winds up being a lifelong friend because you're able to transition your connection to Twitter and respond to each other's tweets.[23] (See the "On Backchannels" section of this chapter for more information.)

Others, including Jonathan Nalder, find Twitter useful but not as engaging as Facebook:

For me, Twitter is really a micro-communications network—short and sharp—mostly in a good way. I've always liked how it encourages brevity. As for what I use it for, I'd say it's 30 percent relational—messages, comments, re-sharing others—and 70 percent publishing the info and links I want to share. Others use it differently, but I had made a deliberate decision early on to build a publishing platform there; this is great for the brand of an ICT [Information and Communication Technologies] educator. This is also fine with me because Facebook is the platform I use for more depth of communicating/relating. Facebook I use 30 percent for publishing, 70 percent for relational activity—and spend more time in the app. Some of this is just due to [the]140/280 characters [limit] in Twitter. The interesting thing is that I also spend more time in Facebook because the response there is way higher despite me having far less "followers" there. Twitter is 12,500, Facebook is about 3,500, and yet I get five times the interaction—likes, comments, sharing—on there. So, [the] positive is Twitter is fast and to the point, but [the] negative is interaction can be fleeting. Facebook is more in-depth interactions, [but the] negative [side], that I and many have long since gotten used to, is you are giving up more information about yourself there because you spend more time there.[24]

—◦◦◦◦—

On Backchannels

A natural extension of using tweet chats to promote social change is to create extended online conversations using backchannels—loosely flowing conversations, via Twitter, that are connected to what is happening during an onsite or online gathering.

There is something playfully engaging and surprisingly productive about taking advantage of backchannel conversations. Friends have described it as the online version of passing notes back and forth during class—a description that very much captures the freewheeling nature of the exchanges that often occur there. I've come to adore backchannels as places where unexpected participants show up and, through their contributions, enrich the experience for participants onsite as well as online. It is, in essence, another variation on the act of creating seamless interactions in the type of global classroom or workspace described in the first chapter of this book.

Establishing and nurturing backchannel conversation is fairly simple and straightforward. Participants agree on a hashtag that will draw participants together through Twitter. They publicize it via Twitter and every other means they have to reach potential participants. They actively draw offsite participants into what is happening onsite by sharing tweets face-to-face with others who are occupying the physical space where the key event—a meeting, rally, conference, or workshop—is occurring, and encouraging onsite participants to respond to their offsite colleagues' comments via Twitter.

The more I explore and engage in the use of backchannel conversation, the more I realize the potential it has for bringing people together. I initially tweeted backchannel comments from conferences I attended, then expanded my participation by tweeting to colleagues who were attending conferences I could not physically attend. A breakthrough moment came a few years ago when the level of response I was providing prompted onsite participants to ask whether I was actually onsite—a thought-provoking experience that reminds me how easy it is to be somewhere without physically being there if I'm thoughtful about the way in which I contribute to the conversations taking place in that blended onsite-online environment.

Anyone interested in a deep dive into the topic will gain plenty by reading Cliff Atkinson's *The Backchannel: How Audiences Are Using Twitter and Social Media and Changing Presentations Forever.*[25] There are also plenty of examples of backchannels in action on my *Building Creative Bridges* blog.[26]

———◦◦◦———

Librarian Elizabeth Myers has seen significant, positive community action inspired by a single tweet (please see Spotlight "On Tweeting, Walking, and Building Community" in this chapter), and David Lee King finds Twitter to be a resource capable of helping him engage with people far beyond the audience he originally envisioned:

> In (I think) 2008, the library had a book challenge. I live-tweeted the board meeting that had a lot of customers sharing, complaining, etc., about the books that were being challenged, and, of course, customers that had the opposing viewpoint. Those tweets actually went international—which was cool! We trended [gained a lot of attention in a short period of time], back when normal people could trend on Twitter.
>
> From that, here's what I picked up on: you have to speak with a neutral voice if you are going about it as a reporter. Otherwise, it won't feel authentic. That's just for "reporting," though. Sharing what other people said during the meeting without making editorial comments about the content. Hard to do! If it's more something that you *are* passionate about, and it's your thing, I think you can definitely *not* be so neutral. You still have to be fair and kind though—apparently also difficult to do in today's odd world.[27]

Twitter has steadily grown to be one of my favorite, most dynamic online tools in terms of how it changes my view of the world and the possibilities I see for fostering positive change. After more than a year of experimenting with Twitter to share resources and engage in rudimentary online exchanges with friends and colleagues all over the world, I unexpectedly took a quantum leap in my perceptions and use of the tool when I became active in the Educational Technology & Media massive open online course (#etmooc), described in the "Elements of Social Media" section of chapter 1. What started as exchanges during live online sessions within the Blackboard platform soon grew into tweets among learners here in the United States as well as in Canada, Australia, and other countries. A tweet in which a co-learner mentioned a resource often led me to spend considerable periods of time reading or viewing the content provided through that link; reflect on the new content by blogging about it and sharing those thoughts with others through a tweet that included a link to the blog article; and often incorporate what I had learned into my own learning offerings face-to-face as well as online with learners I serve. Because I believe that training-teaching-learning is an integral part of fostering social change, I credit Twitter and those with whom I interact through Twitter for much of whatever influence I continue to have among my peers and others in helping transform the face of learning.

ENGAGEMENT THROUGH TWEET CHATS

After initially being drawn into the concept of engaging in live, facilitated conversations through Twitter (tweet chats) as one way of being involved in fostering social change through learning, I joined the online #lrnchat community—a community of trainer-teacher-learner-doers that describes itself on its website as "a place for people interested in the topic of learning who use the social messaging service Twitter to learn from one another and discuss how to help other people learn."[28] Much like the #etmooc community, #lrnchat community members are extremely curious educators who enjoy learning by doing; sharing, through weekly one-hour fast-paced sessions that are generally centered around a current theme of interest in the world in which we work, ideas, and resources we can incorporate into our work; and looking for opportunities to formally and informally collaborate to produce positive change in the communities we serve. The rapid rate at which responses to questions are posted makes it impossible to read and react to every comment made during those dynamically stimulating sessions, so transcripts are posted on the #lrnchat website and conversations continue through replies and retweets long after each session ends.[29] The conversations we have online have that same extended-moment beyond-the-barriers-of-time-and-space nature described throughout this book: what is discussed on #lrnchat often extends into conversations we have when we cross paths at conferences, occasionally see each other over a meal when our travels bring us together, and even through the writing we do.

—◌◌◌—

Pro Tips: Twitter

"Start by following people you are genuinely interested in. Some percentage of those people will follow you back and become part of your community."—Samantha Adams Becker, consultant, whose work with Twitter helped facilitate the growth of a global community of educators promoting change within educational organizations through her work with the New Media Consortium and ShapingEDU

"[B]e picky, if you can, about who you follow. Because a person doesn't have to follow you back on Twitter, there is no harm in not following someone. However, in Facebook—and LinkedIn—that other person needs to accept you. If you can, only accept requests from those you truly want to be connected with."—Jill Hurst-Wahl, Syracuse University, whose use of Twitter helps connect her students with colleagues in the industry in which they currently or plan to work

"Be social, and as relational and human as possible. Show you value others by following, re-tweeting, and commenting. Even choose key accounts in your field and get notifications for them so you can regularly support them. All of this will establish you as a caring community member, meaning when you want to share, you are considered to be a genuine contributor."—Jonathan Nalder, FutureWe, who has parlayed Twitter into a pathway to a global community of educators exploring and promoting positive change in training-teaching-learning

—◌◌◌—

One of my favorite resources describing how tweet chats function is Steve Cooper's Twitter-brief "The Ultimate Guide to Hosting a Tweet Chat," posted on the *Forbes* website on September 30, 2013.[30] In addition to describing tweet chats and offering basic reminders regarding the importance of setting and publicizing times for these online sessions, he reminds readers to be "welcoming and clear" and briefly provides an introduction to free online tools that help facilitators lead engaging, effective sessions. Cayden Mak summarizes his own experiences with tweet chats:

A common Twitter chat format goes like this: the organization host-ing the chat comes up with a list of questions, tweets that list of questions, and expects people to answer. There are a lot of times this doesn't work so well. It gets better if you invite specific guests and they know that they need to pay attention during that time. What we've found works *best* is if you assign each guest a specific question. Like on the radio, dead air on Twitter is a momentum killer, and that's a good way to avoid it.

We generally pick guests by finding people with 1) interesting opinions or perspectives who 2) are savvy users of Twitter and 3) have core audiences that may be interested in our work but not already plugged in and 4) are generally pretty large. "Pretty large" varies by topic; we don't always have guests who have 1 million or even 100,000 followers, but we do try to make sure there are a couple featured guests who have more than 15,000 or 20,000 people who follow them.

The more people you can get to pile onto a hashtag during a live chat, the better. Especially because Twitter doesn't seem to like form tweets, a well-designed chat is a great way to get a hashtag to trend. But that isn't always super useful. Generally, what happens when a hashtag trends is that spam accounts start posting to it and people tweet asking, "What is #this about?" Only if it's part of a larger campaign does it really reach new people.[31]

"Here in Australia, several educators started the #AussieEd hashtag and a weekly chat with specific topics about three years ago," Nalder re-calls.[32] "Many teachers, knowing they need to engage with newer tech-nology and find a personal learning network [PLN]—but getting started can be daunting for teachers here—#AussieEd serves as an easy entry point. Just follow one tag and they can instantly access local ideas and colleagues, so I see that over time it has had quite a large impact on the education community here by providing that."

NEXT STEPS

To gain a better understanding of how the use of Twitter can produce positive opportunities and results for you and those you serve, try either of the following exercises involving a step you are taking to promote a small- or large-scale change in a community with which you work:

- Create a tweet that is designed to be shared and/or elicit responses or actions from those who see it; respond, within Twitter, to any responses you receive to your initial post.
- Go to the ChangeTheWorld-Co community on Slack; initiate or join a discussion on that site in the channel designated for chapter 3; and respond to at least two of the responses your post inspires. (If you have not already joined that community, you can do so by contacting me directly at paul@paulsignorelli.com and including a brief—one-line—description of your interest in learning more about using social media to change the world.)

4

LINKEDIN AND COLLABORATIVE PROJECT-MANAGEMENT TOOLS

Tapping into Business Networks

LinkedIn, a social networking tool created primarily to foster connections between business colleagues and between employers and prospective employees, remains a tremendously underutilized resource available to those interested in drawing upon the skills and resources of their business colleagues in their efforts to foster positive social change. When you see LinkedIn and online social collaboration tools such as Slack and Yammer as potential resources, you increase your ability to effectively engage and communicate with business colleagues who might also be interested in the work you do to change the world—a theme explored throughout this chapter.

LinkedIn, Yammer, Slack, and many other social media collaboration/project-management tools are commonly seen as business resources—tools that can be and occasionally are used by activists, but seldom seem to be used to the full extent possible. A comprehensive paper by Andrew M. Calkins (published in 2013 as a Julie Belle White-Newman MAOL Leadership Award winner at St. Catherine University), "LinkedIn: Key Principles and Best Practices for Online Networking & Advocacy by Nonprofit Organizations,"[1] suggests this has been true for at least half a decade.

This chapter explores the potential of LinkedIn, combined with several other social media collaboration/project-management tools, in reaching and engaging members of your professional/business communities into your efforts to help change the world.

INTRODUCTION TO LINKEDIN

"LinkedIn's value is not so much as a tool to disseminate information to followers, connections, and networks, but as a way to listen, learn and interact with followers, connections, and networks,"[2] Calkins observes in "Key Principles and Best Practices."[3]

While remaining consistent in its foundational strength as a tool connecting people within business communities, LinkedIn is one of many potentially overlooked resources to which you can turn when you want to obtain a snapshot of a potential collaborator's background and interests. It can also help you determine whether you and that potential collaborator have any colleagues in common and, occasionally, help you gather information about a prospective donor for community projects you support. (Please see "On the Strengths and Weaknesses of LinkedIn Connections" elsewhere in this chapter for more information.)

It is not the sort of tool that has—at least so far—attracted significant amounts of money to causes for people interviewed for this book, nor has it attracted significant numbers of active volunteers to get involved in causes. It can, however, produce essential connections and results that put you in a better position to further the causes you do promote and support.

In the same way, posting updates on LinkedIn about the work you and your colleagues are completing can draw more attention to what you are doing and serve as another way to keep that work in the thoughts of those you are attempting to cultivate as supporters and collaborators. Furthermore, its discussion-group function provides an opportunity for open- or closed-group discussions defined and facilitated by those forming and maintaining the groups. It is a way of drawing additional attention to the blog pieces you write to document your work on the theme of community and collaboration. It is a way to provide links to materials you develop and willingly share, under Creative Commons licensing (please see the section on Creative Commons in the next chapter for more information on this copyright-licensing tool), to increase the reach of the work you and your collaborators complete. It is also, as Calkins notes in the concluding section of his paper, "one of many channels to build and nurture interactive relationships and networks."[4]

Topeka and Shawnee County Public Library Digital Services Director David Lee King observes the evolution of LinkedIn:

> LinkedIn has been steadily growing the last few years, which is cool. I've started posting my blog posts there—sharing them there—and I'm getting more people following me there. I actually have a pretty strong readership in LinkedIn right now.
>
> LinkedIn is different—it seems calmer, and not as fast as Twitter, or even Facebook. But you will find different types there, too—people more solidly focused on an industry or cause (thinking nonprofits). So, it can be a great place to start and hold conversations about those passions, again.[5]

"I have seen groups and discussions there that are as good as anywhere, so I definitely think it can be useful for inspiring change—just in a more siloed, professional context that matches the culture there. And, of course, one has to invest the time in creating a genuine presence there first," FutureWe founder Jonathan Nalder says.[6]

"I use it [LinkedIn] the most doing background on program officers I'm working with. Who in movement spaces do they know? Where did they go to school? What are they proud of? It provides a snapshot of what the program officer's key interests and strengths are, and helps me prepare for meetings," 18 Million Rising Executive Director Cayden Mak notes.[7]

—*◦◦◦*—

On the Strengths and Weaknesses of LinkedIn Connections

One of LinkedIn's strengths and weaknesses is its use of designations of first-, second-, and third-level connections. Your first-level connections are those with whom you have formally established a connection through LinkedIn, either by having that person accept a LinkedIn invitation you have sent or by accepting an invitation that person sent to you. Your second-level connections are those directly (as first-level connections) linked to one of your own first-level connections—in theory and in essence, friends of your friends. Your third-level connections are those who are on LinkedIn but have no discernable connection to you or to your own first-level connections.

It is through the expansion of your LinkedIn network through second- and third-level connections that you strengthen your network by connecting to potential collaborators with whom you might otherwise not have a connection. The strength of LinkedIn, then, is to use it to ask your first-level connections for introductions to their own first-level connections, who remain second-level for you.

In an ideal world—one in which every LinkedIn user actually had strong personal connections with his or her own first-level connections—this would be tremendously helpful. You would see someone you want to meet through LinkedIn, recognize you have a shared connection, and ask the shared connection to make the introduction. What often happens, however, is that you will find that you and your LinkedIn colleagues have only the most tenuous of connections to many of those first-level LinkedIn connections. This can happen naturally as you accept LinkedIn invitations from colleagues in a professional organization to which you belong but whom you have not personally met face-to-face or online before receiving the LinkedIn invitation. The problem this can cause occurs when you attempt to connect directly to one of your second-level connections and initiate your invitation with a mention of that contact's own first-level connection—who may never, beyond accepting a LinkedIn invitation, have actually had any significant contact with the person to whom you are reaching out. The solution here is obvious: if you are going to send a LinkedIn invitation to a second-level connection, take the time to reach out to the person who is apparently your link to your prospect and check to see how well your first-level contact knows that second-level contact.

As in all social media interactions, a little extra effort up front can produce wonderful results while avoiding potentially embarrassing results.

INTRODUCTION TO COLLABORATION/PROJECT-MANAGEMENT TOOLS: SLACK, TRELLO, AND YAMMER

There are numerous social media tools designed to foster online collaboration for project-management purposes, Vartika Kashyap confirms in "28 Best Slack Alternatives [in 2020] for Team Communication (You Cannot Live Without)."[8] These are tools that you can easily adapt to your efforts to foster social change when you embrace the idea that your work involves a high degree of project management.

Three that are currently popular are Slack, Trello, and Yammer. When effectively facilitated, they can create safe and engaging online workspaces for conversations among members of action-oriented groups. The tools thrive or die as resources depending upon the levels of engagement their participants offer and the presence of first-rate facilitators within the communities using those tools. And those tools allow for community members to shape and organize the conversations and planning through the organizational skills of the participants themselves as they create various workspaces—"channels" or "lists"—within the overall platforms based on the changing interests and needs of the members of those communities.

When users join those communities willingly, with strong commitments to the goals the communities are pursuing, the tools quickly fade into the background and the work being pursued flourishes. Members of well-run Slack, Trello, and Yammer communities tend to support one another very effectively by responding quickly to questions posed by new participants who have questions about how the tools work. There are also plenty of resources (e.g., Jessica Kerr's blog post "Effective Use of Slack";[9] Lydia Dishman's *Fast Company* article "Best Practices from the Most Active Slack Users";[10] and Jory MacKay's "How to Use Slack Effectively: 25 Slack Settings and Features That Will Save Your Focus"[11] for the *RescueTime* blog) available online to guide participants through the learning curve that accompanies initial use of an unfamiliar tool.

Slack, Trello, Yammer, and other similar tools "can work well in more of a group setting," King suggests. "If the group is already established, it's a great place to hold conversations with just that group. Much less cluttered and distracting than, say a Facebook group that also has links and notifications of other things going on all the time. So, they can be really useful, more focused tools."[12]

Mak observes the usefulness of Slack in his situation of working with staff located in various parts of the United States, rather than having everyone working side by side in a central office:

> [Slack is] really helpful since we're remote—we can easily share stuff—and it keeps it out of the inbox and prevents having to re-explain stuff to teammates who maybe didn't get cc-d on a thread. Our board members are in there, and so are our long-term volunteers. We haven't used Slack in the large-scale way that some people are using Slack—our application is a little more like a traditional office than anything else. But it's a good place for conversation and to hash out ideas about stuff because it *is* so closed and safe. . . . Doing the work we're doing now, remotely and with a meaningfully diverse team, would have been basically impossible at our budget size like 10 years ago. That's a big deal, especially when the impact a small team can have is already super outsized with the Internet.[13]

ENGAGING THROUGH SLACK TO BUILD (OR REBUILD) COMMUNITY

The sudden, unexpected closing of the New Media Consortium (NMC) by its board of directors in December 2017 was shocking to educators promoting positive change in learning organizations and communities around the world.[14] This was a consortium that, through its work from its inception in 1993, had established itself as a globally recognized resource for anyone interested in tracking innovations and identifying key trends and challenges in educational technology, with a goal of promoting positive change among those familiar with its work. More importantly, the information captured and provided freely online through NMC's annual, biennial, and occasional one-time special reports through its Horizon Project fostered positive change in learning environments within higher education, the K–12 sector, community colleges, museums, libraries, and other educational organizations whose members used what they learned from the reports. Each new edition of an NMC Horizon Report was downloaded by hundreds of thousands of readers—the first two Horizon reports for libraries, in 2014 and 2015, were downloaded more than 1.8 million times[15] —and discussions and actions generated by the content in those reports continued at NMC conferences, in a variety of online settings including webinars produced by NMC, and in numerous formal and informal gatherings sponsored and facilitated by NMC community members.

—————————

On Connecting LinkedIn to Other Social Media Tools

Colleagues are consistently passionate—and not necessarily in agreement—in their opinions about whether to post content, directly and unaltered, from one social media account (e.g., LinkedIn) to another (e.g., Twitter). Social media platforms offer a variety of ways to share content from one platform to another, and those interested in connecting their LinkedIn accounts to another account will—when it is possible to automate that process—find simple, straightforward guidance through the LinkedIn Help center.[16]

There is, in general, agreement that personalizing content on a specific topic from platform to platform is a good practice to follow—particularly because each tool has its own possibilities and limitations. This was obvious when Twitter had a limit of 140 characters per post (until that limit was doubled in 2017 to 280 characters per post). LinkedIn, on the other hand, had a much larger limit, and Facebook had no limit beyond how long a post you could expect your Facebook friends to read before abandoning you to read a more concise, enticing offering.

Automated cross-posting—the act of setting up your accounts so that something posted in LinkedIn, for example, is duplicated on Twitter—can help you more effectively use the limited time you have for maintaining a cohesive, productive, effective social media presence that keeps you in touch with your current and prospective supporters.

Cross-posting automatically—as opposed to adapting content used on one platform for use on another—does, however, come at a cost. Knowing that some of your LinkedIn posts will also appear on Twitter, you will find it useful to incorporate hashtags and shortened URLs created through the use of the free online TinyURL or Bitly services (practices that are very familiar to Twitter users, but somewhat confusing to those who only use LinkedIn or Facebook because, to the uninitiated, those hashtags and shortened URLs appear to be nothing more than gibberish) into your LinkedIn posts. This might, however, confuse those in LinkedIn who are unfamiliar with what is commonly seen in Twitter and leave them feeling that some elements of your posts are indecipherable. You will have to decide whether the small amount of antagonism those hashtags and shortened URLs foster, compared to the benefits of reaching a much larger and receptive audience, makes the use of cross-posting worth pursuing. You might also be inspired to reach your Facebook colleagues in more personalized ways on issues that are best served by posts created solely for viewing on Facebook, or by simply going into your Facebook account and lightly editing the posts that you initiate in LinkedIn or Twitter.

———◦◦◦———

To imagine a world without the community of innovative forward-thinking educators NMC had fostered was impossible for many members of that community, so several asked a question that has proved to be transformative: What can we do, in a post-NMC world, to retain this tremendous blended (onsite-online) community of learning activists? It took only a few days of conversations with a rapidly expanding group of colleagues to see the obvious: participants were part of a global community firmly rooted in and comfortable with online communication via social media tools. They had already routinely used wikis, Twitter, Facebook, and numerous other tools to engage in conversations and complete their work as learning activists with NMC and a variety of other organizations. If they could quickly find a tool that would make it easy to have the conversations needed to carry this community beyond the safe haven NMC had provided for more than two decades, they might be able to avoid losing what they saw as NMC's greatest asset: the community of teacher-trainer-learner-doers itself.

Those three days of intense exchanges rapidly produced an option more than a dozen initial participants agreed to pursue: Slack. The initial step, completed overnight, involved establishing a "Beyond the Horizon" Slack community. Invitations to join that Slack community began going out almost immediately to colleagues within the extensive NMC community. Within a few days, seventy-five former NMC volunteers and staff members had joined and were engaged in proposing options to keep the community intact; the number of active community members increased to nearly two hundred within two weeks. Within two months, the community had set dates for a small, informal onsite "Unconference for Dreamers, Doers, and Drivers Shaping the Future of Learning" to parallel, in a small way, what NMC's annual conference used to provide. The unconference, with more than a hundred participants from several countries, was held on an Arizona State University campus in April 2018.[17] A new project name for educational technology reports was established (FOEcast,[18] to playfully suggest a Future of Education Forecast series going beyond what the community had produced through NMC), and a full week of online activities at the end of February and in early March 2018 helped define what FOEcast would be producing. The ShapingEDU community had established an online site within the Arizona State University website by mid-May 2018, and unconference organizers issued a brief "communique" defining "10 Actions to Shape the Future of Education"[19]—a clear sign that new groups were rising out of the NMC community while EDUCAUSE, which purchased the NMC assets, continued to provide a setting for the continuing work of this vibrant community of learning activists.

"As someone who is using Slack more and more in my professional life, I think it is a wonderful example of real-time, private conversations being facilitated online," Samantha Adams Becker, who frequently facilitates ShapingEDU onsite and online activities, says. "You can build and mobilize a community there. This has been the case with the Beyond [the] Horizon community, where new users are introducing themselves every day and people are openly sharing their hopes and dreams for ensuring the spirit of the NMC lives on."[20]

ENGAGING THROUGH JIVE TO CREATE COMMUNITY AND CHANGE

Jeff Merrell, Associate Director of Northwestern University's Master's Program in Learning and Organizational Change, leads his learners toward and through social change by incorporating the use of the Jive social media collaboration tool into the work they do together.

Through his course that "explores enterprise social networking technology and its impact on organizational knowledge and organizational learning in the workplace," he sets out to incorporate prototyping, class projects, and business cases into the learning process.[21] The results are often as much personal as professional and offer fascinating insights into the way social collaboration tools themselves foster personal change through the act of using those tools. Merrell explains this idea further:

> [Using Jive], we intentionally tried to create more of a workplace feel for our program, rather than using an academic LMS [learning management system]. Jive is an enterprise social network platform that allows us to have dialogue and interactions within courses (privately) and across our entire community of learners, faculty, staff and alum. All within one space—and it very much looks like a corporate social intranet.
>
> So, in my course, I have the advantage of leveraging our platform to talk about the issues of enterprise social media. But we also look at things like Yammer, Slack and sometimes other platforms—Chatter—to get a sense of what the field looks like.

Merrell creatively provides varying levels of privacy for his learners when encouraging them to interact via Jive or any other social media tool. There sometimes are discussions that are only open and visible to the instructor and the learners; there are others that "'leak out' to the larger community" beyond the physical and virtual walls of his classrooms. And there are some conversations—as was the case in the Personal Learning Network massive open online course (#PLNMOOC) I took with Merrell a few years ago—that extend from the physical classrooms with his Northwestern University students to the online community Merrell facilitated for those of us not in any way formally affiliated with Northwestern.

In his "Revisiting: A Critical Pedagogy for Organizational Learning?" blog post in January 2018, Merrell writes about a "kind of collision between the 'outside' social world and internal organizational world," a theme we explored during our interview for this book.[22]

> Two of the most powerful "open" discussions we've had within our community—open to the entire community, but not open to the public—have been about being a Muslim (visiting student) in the U.S. and the challenges of being a female in tech. In both cases, these are very strong, female leaders who opened these discussions. And each was spurred by some outside event. Each also said they

would not write what they wrote anywhere else than within the community we created. And each, also, were very savvy social media users—blogging, on Twitter, etc. And the discussion threads—and related conversations outside of the online space—I found productive for the community as a whole. That was also the general sense of the leaders in this program, and from what I could gather, the community itself. . . .

Positive change coming from it? Not sure I can point to the lives of Muslim students being any "safer" or that women in tech are better off now. But there is a history here that now proves and demonstrates that our [course] community . . . can take on these topics and explore them and learn from them.[23]

———◦◦◦———

Pro Tips: LinkedIn and Slack

"I think 'intentional design' is needed for the use of such platforms for social change. It's similar to how you can't just throw people in a room face-to-face and expect good things to happen with no planning. [Ask yourself] 'what will you ask of people once they're in the room? How will you organize side conversations as more people enter?'"—Samantha Adams Becker, consultant, who incorporates images into her various social media posts on a variety of accounts

"Be willing to create rules of engagement. Who will enforce the rules? Although you may never need to use the rules, it can be helpful to have them. And remind people on occasion what the rules are. If possible, have the rules sent out to newbies automatically."—Jill Hurst-Wahl, whose work creating guidelines for online communication has facilitated productive engagement among members of nonprofit organizations she has joined and served

"In smaller-scale communities, with a community manager or facilitator who maybe speaks the professional language of the community, you can begin to create a safe place to share. You can create norms that (hopefully) prevent and mitigate the risk of unproductive comments."—Jeff

Merrell, Northwestern University, whose work with Jive and other collaboration tools fosters transformation among his learners and the organizations and communities they ultimately serve

—*◦/◦/◦*—

Stepping back long enough to provide a comparison between how these social media tools connect to one another, Merrell suggests that "LinkedIn is about your 'brand.' So right there, you are screwed unless you as an individual are seeking to be branded as social activist. But I would suspect—maybe I am wrong—that someone with that mindset would find LinkedIn just not a fit. It's about people trying to create a professional brand in the traditional corporate model. Slack and Yammer, and similar [tools] allow more co-construction of 'space.' A group of social activists, within an organization, could easily start up a Slack community of trusted peers, etc.; set norms for participation; and maybe have a go of it."[24]

Merrell's work with his learners clearly demonstrates that this level of effort doesn't just contribute to the results you can achieve in fostering positive social change. It also strengthens the connections, productivity, and trust within the groups contributing to those changes through the synchronous and asynchronous exchanges they make possible in your ever-evolving social media environments.

NEXT STEPS

To gain a better understanding of how the use of LinkedIn, Slack, Yammer, and other online collaboration and project-management tools can produce positive opportunities and results for you and those you serve, try either of the following exercises involving a step you are taking to promote a small- or large-scale change in a community with which you work:

- Create a post that is designed to be shared and/or elicit responses or actions from those who see it; respond, within the social media platform you have chosen, to any responses you receive to your initial post.

- Go to the ChangeTheWorld-Co community on Slack; initiate or join a discussion on that site in the channel designated for chapter 4; and respond to at least two of the responses your post inspires. (If you have not already joined that community, you can do so by contacting me directly at paul@paulsignorelli.com and including a brief—one-line—description of your interest in learning more about using social media to change the world.)

5

PICTURING CHANGE

Instagram, Snapchat, and Flickr

Instagram, Snapchat, and Flickr are among the popular image-centric social media platforms available to you to reach your colleagues and supporters with compelling photographs and brief, engaging bits of text designed to inspire positive action. In this chapter, you will see how activists addressing a variety of challenges and issues are incorporating those tools into their tool kits.

Ephemeral moments, briefly captured and shared through imagery, are at the heart of Snapchat—a social media platform used by nearly 75 percent of teens in America.[1] It is a tool that is designed to playfully combine text captions and imagery through a here-today, gone-tomorrow approach. What you post there is generally meant to last no longer than twenty-four hours before disappearing. The tremendously world-changing impact a Snapchat post can have, however, became clear in early 2018, when a teenaged Snapchat user captured the horrendous moments of the mass shooting of students, by a former student, at Marjory Stoneman Douglas High School in Parkland, Florida.[2]

This was a snap that did not—and will not—disappear. Copied and reposted online and included in mainstream media coverage of the tragedy, it has taken on a life of its own. It was part of a student-driven online social media presence that helped spur the March for Our Lives (#MarchForOurLives) protest movement that has attracted participation from students and adults in more than eight hundred cities worldwide[3] and its companion initiatives, Vote for Our Lives (#VoteForOur-Lives) and #NeverAgain. Within one month of the shooting, these movements had produced gun-control legislation in Oregon[4] and Flori-da[5] unlike any that previously came out of years of fruitless conversations between those in favor of somehow limiting access to guns and those who firmly believe that the Second Amendment to the United States Constitution provides absolute, uncontrolled access to guns.

Watching that snap or looking at March for Our Lives images on Instagram[6] and Flickr[7] takes you to the heart of one of the most divisive debates in America today. You don't just see people affected by an issue seeking some sort of positive resolution: you see the issue playing out in sometimes spiteful, vicious comments between those who find themselves on opposite sides of a debate that was producing few concrete results—until that snap went viral. The students became advocates with often very sophisticated approaches to the social (and mainstream) media tools available to them, and they joined the voices of those insisting that "enough is enough" and that a positive response to the most awful of situations had to come sooner rather than later.

The fact that Snapchat was the initial vehicle for providing painfully jarring intimate glimpses into another tragedy unfolding was probably something that the creators of Snapchat could never have predicted when they made a platform for capturing and briefly disseminating ephemeral moments.

SAB Creative & Consulting President Samantha Adams Becker weighs in on how social media evolves beyond its original intent, for better or for worse:

> I don't think Mark Zuckerberg ever dreamed that Facebook would be involved in presidential election scandals and the fake-news cycle. Nor do I think that Snapchat leadership pictured teens snapping violent and traumatic injury in the midst of a horrific crisis. It's not necessarily something you envision from the get-go, but it makes sense that social networks would be effective vehicles for spreading news, exposing real-life events in progress, etc. But there can definitely be backlash. I'm thinking about the Logan Paul YouTube scandal from a couple months ago, where he showed footage from a suicide.[8] People are rightfully concerned that social media can glamorize the tragic. It's a very delicate balance and there is a fine line between sharing something that spurs positive action vs. negative

reactions. The in-situ experience of social media means that people aren't always thinking before they post—and they can be greatly penalized for that or end up inspiring the wrong kind of action.

I don't have a solution for how and where to draw the line, but we could use more guidance around that and more ways to educate forthcoming generations and provide proper digital literacy training.[9]

—◦◦◦—

On Creative Commons and the Use of Others' Images

When using images posted in Flickr and other photo-sharing social media platforms, please remember that not all of them are free for the taking. Unauthorized use of someone else's photos can have the unpleasant consequences that accompany any copyright violation—including demands for payment from those who actually own or represent those who own those images. (A caveat: beware of any unexpected contact from someone demanding payment for an image you used. Before responding to that sort of unwelcome demand, contact a copyright attorney, if necessary, to determine whether your use of the image is covered under Fair Use doctrine guidelines.[10])

Creative Commons, an American nonprofit organization that helps the producers of creative works determine how many or few copyright restrictions they want to place on the use and modification of their work, provides you with information regarding any restrictions that have been placed on the use of an image you are interested in using. It is also a useful service when determining how you want your own posted images to be used and disseminated.

"The Creative Commons copyright licenses and tools forge a balance inside the traditional 'all rights reserved' setting that copyright law creates," the organization explains on its website. "Our tools give everyone from individual creators to large companies and institutions a simple, standardized way to grant copyright permissions to their creative work. The combination of our tools and our users is a vast and growing digital commons, a pool of content that can be copied, distributed, edited, remixed, and built upon, all within the boundaries of copyright law."[11]

Each image on Flickr generally is accompanied by a description of the type of license that has been applied to it. The most generous of the six licenses—the Attribution 2.0 Generic license—allows you to modify and distribute an image in any way you care to as long as you provide the attribution the owner of the image requests. The most restrictive license—Attribution-NonCommercial-NoDerivs—allows for downloading and sharing of images without alteration, with attribution, and for non-commercial use only.

———〰〰〰———

Briefly tracing the early, rapid growth of #MarchForOurLives provides another strong reminder that specific social media platforms do not operate in a vacuum; they are part of an overall combination of traditional and relatively new media formats available to those who want to take the small- and large-scale steps that can lead to changing the world. #MarchForOurLives at least in part grew rapidly because those Snapchat images inspired action in a variety of ways: through mainstream and cable news programs; postings on other social media platforms including Facebook, Twitter, Flickr, Instagram, and YouTube; fundraising efforts coordinated by the nonprofit March for Our Lives Action Fund[12] and others; and the personalization of the story through Parkland student-activists including Emma Gonzalez and David Hogg.[13] In fact, that personalization draws us in and inspires us to action through the power of storytelling—through Snapchat, Twitter, Facebook, YouTube, and book-length explorations that bring these stories to people who might otherwise be overwhelmed and unable to see that the road from observer to activist can be traveled in many different ways and in relatively short periods of time. David Hogg and his sister, Lauren, appear to understand this implicitly: less than six months after the shooting in Parkland, they were able to publish #NeverAgain, a call to action published by Random House Trade Paperbacks.

This chapter explores the use of image-based social media platforms to promote positive social change in your communities and suggests some of the ways they can be interwoven with other platforms useful to activists.

INTRODUCTION TO SNAPCHAT

Snapchat, like so many other social media tools, remains very much a work in progress. Its early evolution carried it from being a service where images and short videos were posted for brief periods of time to one in which images could be connected to tell stories. Live storytelling through video soon followed, and the "Discover" function was introduced to help users find and share content from a wide-range of Internet sites. A major redesign of the service in 2017 was poorly received, reportedly causing the valuation of the company to drop by more than a billion dollars,[14] so much of the redesign was rolled back a few months later.

It is also a tool with potentially world-changing impact,[15] as the reach of the Snapchat video from Parkland suggests. Ad Council Vice President of Media Laurie Keith, for example, has written about how she works with Snapchat to "build social impact partnerships that raise awareness of critical issues [including cyber bullying, AIDs prevention, and hunger prevention] in America."[16] Staff members at Fenton, a public relations firm focusing on social change campaigns (including some involving climate change, public health, race and gender equality, and human rights), have used Snapchat for a Unicef campaign to raise awareness of missing children who were abducted by members of Boko Haram; a World Wildlife Fund of Denmark campaign about endangered species; campaigns highlighting the plights of Syrian refugees; and others.[17] University of Denver PhD candidate (at the time) Paige Alfonzo, writing for *American Libraries* magazine, documents library-based examples that can serve as inspiration to anyone interested in creating awareness of various activities: snaps sent from events in progress, snaps promoting upcoming events, and snaps designed to share news with supporters.[18]

—————

On Internet Memes and Infopics

One way in which images and brief snippets of text come together in social media platforms is through the use of Internet memes—humorous or satirical combinations of words and images sometimes designed to provoke thought and social action.[19] A variety of tools make the production of these "infopics" fairly easy to produce. FutureWe Founder Jonathan Nalder explains these further:

> I did a lot of work around making and training people in Infopics a while back. Tony Vincent and I coined the phrase, and he has produced this great page: https://learninginhand.com/infopics.[20] It basically means to pair an image with text to tell a story or message. At the time, it was something new to most people, and the general idea is pretty common and accessible now, but still useful as a way to add to one's visual messaging online. The fact that it is a well-used method now is a sign it's an idea that has spread and is having an impact. It's not an example of a conscious effort to create a community, though, but of a tool available to support communities in general. . . .
>
> I'd made a few playing around as I do, and being a photographer and poet/writer, it was always something I'd try. Of course, there is a trick—like with Twitter when it was 140 characters—of keeping the text succinct. And then Tony, who has done amazing work supporting teachers and producing resources for years, was also interested in offering training on its potential, so we chatted on what would be a name to describe it so people would "get it," and that's what we came up with. I have also made video versions that are like fifteen secs and have the text over moving images.[21]

—

INTRODUCTION TO INSTAGRAM

Even the most cursory of Internet searches produces stunning examples of how Instagram users are attempting to foster awareness of issues at local, national, and international levels in the hope that awareness is a first step toward positive social change.[22] Devorah Rose, writing for *Vice* magazine, highlights Instagram accounts drawing attention to causes ranging from gender equality to the plight of polar bears.[23] A *Founder's Guide* article highlights nine Instagram accounts, including those maintained by the World Wildlife Fund and Everyday Climate Change, devoted to calling attention to humanitarian causes.[24] A *Dazed* article about "activists taking down the establishment one shot at a time" introduces readers to a variety of Instagram accounts on themes including "homeless youth, LGBTQ youth, and other vulnerable populations," Black Lives Matter, and the #StopRapeEducate campaign.[25]

Your posts on Snapchat do not have to be momentous; innocuous posts on Instagram can sometimes produce opportunities that spur small- or large-scale action toward fostering change. Topeka and Shawnee County Public Library Digital Services Director David Lee King recalls how this has been true for him.

> My library definitely connects to customers using Instagram. Here's one example from Monday. We were closed on Monday for our annual staff day, and posted an Instagram message. One of our customers left a comment, asking, of all things, if it was true that Trump's federal budget was cutting funding to libraries. So, I had to do some research, and answer appropriately. I said something about the federal budget as it stands now plans to cut things like IMLS [Institute of Museum and Library Services], etc., and briefly explained that that would affect libraries.
>
> It was hard to answer in an Instagram comment. But it worked! The person thanked us for the comment, and said something like, "Now I know that I need to call my congressman to get that back in the budget!"[26]

—◄Θ/Θ/Θ►—

Pro Tips: Snapchat, Instagram, and Flickr

"If you create an image or video for one platform, it's becoming easier to instantly share it on another, which speaks to the 'design once, deploy everywhere' philosophy. Content can be repurposed, which is one way it can go viral."—Samantha Adams Becker, consultant, who uses images in a variety of social media platforms

"Take your own photos, rather than relying on the photos of others. . . . That way, you're telling the visual story that you want to tell."—Jill Hurst-Wahl, who incorporates her own images into blog posts, Facebook postings, and other online work

"Decide on your message and main topics or main points. And then find images that support or illustrate those points. . . . You are looking for visual and emotional tugs to reinforce those points or topics. If it can be done with a bit of humor, so much the better; people remember things they laugh at."—David Lee King, author of *Face2Face: Using Face-book, Twitter, and Other Social Media Tools to Create Great Customer Connections*

———*୬୬୬*———

INTRODUCTION TO FLICKR

The use of Flickr, one of several social media platforms for posting photographs that can be viewed and shared within user-determined sets of controls and restrictions (please see Spotlight "On Creative Commons and the Use of Others' Images" in this chapter), can extend far beyond the act of capturing an event through imagery. It can also be a way of drawing people into an organization's campaigns or even routine meetings, as illustrated by the approach taken by The Poor People's Campaign, a "national call for moral revival."[27]

"When they have a mass meeting, [they] ask people at the start of the meeting to snap a photo of the event and to share it on social media immediately," Syracuse University Associate Professor of Practice Jill Hurst-Wahl notes. "I find that a really interesting and useful strategy. They want to call attention to what they are doing. . . . So, what comes to mind is that if I'm curious about who is at that event and how it is structured, the photos will tell me that. I've used photos to learn more about who was in the room, how many people were in the room, etc. If photos are shared in real time, then they might pique the interest of online participants—'hey, there is a photo'—who might then pay attention to the text interactions."[28]

Hurst-Wahl has also found that interactions among users on Flickr can produce unexpectedly positive results. She has occasionally reached out to people whose images she wanted to incorporate into work she does online, and later found conversations blossoming when she met those Flickr colleagues face-to-face in settings ranging from conferences to airports. Her successes—some planned, some serendipitous—remind you that a diligent, creative, focused, and long-term approach to incorporating your work into Flickr, the platforms discussed in this chapter, and other social media services including Twitter and Facebook can carry your work far beyond those initial posts and contribute to the overall reach of the small-, medium-, and large-scale campaigns you create, promote, and manage.

NEXT STEPS

To gain a better understanding of how the use of social media tools based on effective imagery can produce positive opportunities and results for you and those you serve, try either of the following exercises involving a step you are taking to promote a small- or large-scale change in a community with which you work:

- Create a post that is designed to be shared and/or elicit responses or actions from those who see it; respond, within the social media platform (e.g., Snapchat or Instagram) you have chosen, to any responses you receive.
- Go to the ChangeTheWorld-Co community on Slack; initiate or join a discussion on that site in the channel designated for chapter 5; and respond to at least two of the responses your post inspires. (If you have not already joined that community, you can do so by contacting me directly at paul@paulsignorelli.com and including a brief—one-line—description of your interest in learning more about using social media to change the world.)

6

BLOGGING FOR SOCIAL CHANGE

Blogging can be a key pathway to sharing your story with current and prospective members of your community. The combination of text, images, videos, and links to useful and inspiring resources helps you engage and motivate your colleagues. This chapter explores key elements of incorporating blogging into your change-the-world tool kit.

If you have the mistaken impression that you can't blog, you might want to check out Hannah Alper's *Call Me Hannah* blog for inspiration.[1] Starting it when she was nine years old and driven by a desire to be involved in promoting positive change in the environment, this extraordinary Canadian—who is seventeen years old at the time of this writing—found her voice, her audience, and an opportunity to grow in ways that continue to have an impact through her work as an activist, blogger, motivational speaker, and author.

Alper stands out as a wonderful example of someone whose blogging and other social media endeavors are part of an overall tool kit that helps her reach her audience in world-changing ways. Building upon the success of her blog, she has published a book (*Momentus: Small Acts, Big Change*[2]) comprised of interviews with nineteen other activists. She gains further attention for the causes she promotes by doing interviews for print publications and television stations. She travels as a presenter as well as someone who documents the changes she is promoting. Through all of these efforts, she conducts herself in ways that channel the attention she is receiving into attention and information about the causes she supports.

There are obvious elements to notice in her blog. She consistently displays a simple, effective use of language. She projects a sincere approach to the topics she tackles as her interests continue to evolve. She includes engaging photographs that help establish a persona that flows through all her work. Most importantly, she provides consistent calls to action so readers know they are being invited to do more than consume what she writes, and she responds to the comments they post; they are her partners in creating positive change in a world about which they care deeply.

Tracing the ever-evolving arc of her work is easy, given the record of those interests she continues to explore through her blog. One of her earliest pieces, "Be More Eco-Friendly for $10 and 10 Minutes," documents the efforts she made with her mother to create recycling bins in their home to reduce the amount of garbage they were adding to local landfills, and even this early post—written when she was nine—reached out to readers with the hope that "you might try this too" and an invitation to those readers to share their own ideas about recycling.[3] Within a few years, she was advocating for positive responses to bullying and actively involved in other WE Movement initiatives that are community-based, national, and global in their reach[4] while also continuing to advocate for small actions that contribute to large-scale environmental change through recycling, composting, and even engaging in impromptu efforts to pick up trash from her local schoolyard. That September 20, 2015 post on her blog continued to feature encouragement to her readers—"I always say little things add up to make a big difference"—along with simple, concrete actions her readers could take if they, too, wanted to be part of the effort to make communities cleaner.[5] Other posts have covered themes as varied as the March for Our Lives activities in March 2018, the continuing decline of global bee populations, mental health issues (particularly in terms of how they affect people within her own peer group), and using social media in advocacy.

What remains most striking in her writing and serves as a tremendous reminder to you about an approach you can pursue in your own blogging for social change, however, is her willingness to be inspiringly transparent. A piece in her book that was also posted on her blog, for example, reads as a from-the-heart admission that while she loves what she does and remains in awe of many of the people she continues to meet through her work, it isn't easy and it does take a toll. In that "It's

Not Always Sunshine and Rainbows" post, she reflects on how she is "often mocked and put down" by classmates; how the negative comments make her question her choices and lower her self-esteem; and how the work she has chosen to pursue causes her to "miss out on everyday things like clubs and student council." And, as usual, she concludes with the suggestion that her readers—her fellow travelers on the journey she (and you) have obviously chosen to take—remember why they have chosen that particular journey, "and then, keep going."[6]

This, then, is part of the power of blogging to change the world. It provides you with a chance to compose your thoughts before sharing them with members and prospective members of your community of support. It provides for plenty of opportunities for engagement if you are willing to court and respond to comments from members of your community. It allows you to build a body of work to which you can return as your own interests develop. After all, as so many writers have said, there are times when if you want to read something, you have to write it yourself—and then hope that it leads to the small-, medium-, and large-scale changes you are attempting to foster.

INTRODUCTION TO BLOGGING

Blogging, as you saw from the summary of Hannah Alper's work, can be a key pathway to telling your story. It offers you a chance to be as brief or as lengthy as your efforts require you to be. It provides a way to seamlessly and effectively combine words with photographs and videos. It allows you to provide readers with as little or as much as they want from you because they can quickly skim or read a post from start to finish or spend considerably longer periods of time exploring links you embed to other resources throughout your article. And, when done engagingly, it inspires conversations in ways you initially cannot anticipate. All you have to do is write.

The idea of writing for an audience is, of course, appealing and natural to some—and absolutely frightening and overwhelming to others. If you are already a proficient writer who knows how to transform ideas into effective, engaging prose, consider yourself lucky and carry that knowledge into your blog posts. If you want to blog but don't have a lot of experience writing for publication, here are five tips to help you reach current and prospective members of your change-the-world community:

Picture your audience—an individual or group of people interested in what you are saying—and write to that person or group. One of the quickest ways to lose an audience (or fail to attract one in the first place) is to write without an audience in mind. As you consider the blogs that keep you coming back for more, you can probably see that the writers of those blogs seem to be speaking directly to you regardless of whether their blogs are written in first-, second-, or third-person voice. They draw you in because they make you feel that they care about you, have something to say to you specifically, and invite you to join them in taking whatever action they are writing to support. Emulating that example sets you up for success as you develop and work with your community through blogging.

Be simple and clear, with a goal in mind. Those who use blogging as a form of journaling, sharing personal observations with a larger audience in the hope that those observations resonate and provide a pleasurable reading experience, are working toward one goal. When you begin or continue to refine your efforts to incorporate blogging into your social-media tool kit and reach out to others interested in advancing the positive social changes you are seeking, you are doing at least three things: (1) identifying a problem that you hope also concerns them; (2) proposing a course of action that attempts to address that problem in a way that appeals to those to whom you are writing; and (3) inviting levels of engagement with your readers in the hope that you can work with them to achieve the goals you all want to achieve. Leaving out any of these key elements undercuts your efforts to change the world in small and large ways and produces missed opportunities rather than results.

Recognize that your first draft does not have to be—and will not be—perfect. It is the rare writer who produces a polished piece on a first attempt. Acknowledging that writing in an inspiring way takes time, effort, and persistence can help you overcome the inner critic that stops so many potential writers from reaching, interacting with, and fostering action among those who read and react to their work. Seeing that awful first draft slowly—and sometimes painfully—take on the shape you instinctively know it can assume is just the first of many rewards that come from blogging. For some, the process becomes easier over time in the same way that any consistently sustained effort does; for others, writing remains a chore—but one that produces results well worth the effort. Regardless of how the process works for and feels to you, it becomes worthwhile if it helps you reach the goals you have set for yourself and members of your community in your efforts to change the world.

Rewrite your piece as many times as necessary to achieve the structure, tone, and clarity that will make a reader want to stay with you and be inspired to take the action you are promoting. Acknowledging that first drafts are rarely perfect is one step; remaining committed to refining that draft until it meets the high standards you and your collaborators set for one another is an entirely different matter. It is an oft-stated truism that if you want to be a writer, you need to write on a regular basis. Seeing writing as a process rather than a just-sit-down-and-let-the-good-words-flow endeavor can help you through those times when writing for your blog is the last thing you want to be doing.

Before posting your article, share it with someone you trust—someone with the same commitment to clear, engaging communication and action that you yourself hold. This can be a difficult part of the process because it can be painful and frustrating to hear someone tell you that a piece you adore and seems to you to be the best you have ever produced misses the mark a bit—or a lot. It can also be very helpful in that constructive criticism from someone who shares your commitment to great writing and positive action is one of the greatest gifts a writer can receive. You ultimately have final say over what you post on your own blog, and you ultimately bear responsibility for and take the heat for those posts that draw critical response—which, by the way, is going to be common if you are attempting to work around the most difficult and controversial issues facing communities today. Having the support of a writer-editor you trust can help you through some of the roughest responses you are going to receive; having a thick skin is also important as you incorporate blogging into your social media tool kit.

Here's a bonus tip I have learned—and relearned—from many writers whose work I admire:

Read your piece aloud, to yourself, before posting it. Hearing how the words flow when spoken, and paying particular attention to those moments when you inadvertently "read" something that is not actually on your screen or the printed page, helps you identify the rough spots and identify better phrasing than you had produced up to that moment. Reading aloud also helps you identify awkward phrases. It helps you identify sentences that go on much longer than they should; if you are running out of breath trying to read an entire sentence, that is a not-to-be-ignored indication that it probably needs to be broken into at least two separate sentences. Finally, it helps you hear ideas that do not flow as nicely—or even poetically—as they could or should as you work toward transforming your thoughts into the thoughts of those you hope will soon embrace and act upon them. There is a rhythm to first-rate writing that is not at all apparent until you actually hear it; reading aloud makes you much more conscious of the power of beautifully crafted language, and it entices you into using it to the benefit of the causes and the people you are attempting to serve.

〰〰〰

On Tagging Content

Tagging—attaching a consistent set of keywords to your blog posts[7]—is one of the many ways you can help readers find your content. It requires planning, consistency in terms of the vocabulary you use as tags, and a commitment to knowing your audience—the interests members of that audience have, the vocabulary they are most comfortable using, and the terms they are most likely to use when looking for online resources, including the content you provide through your blog.

The tags you use will change over time. Part of this evolution of your personal taxonomy comes naturally as you become more aware of terms your audience uses; you develop this awareness by seeing which keywords members of your audience frequently use in their own communications, blog posts, tweets, and other online interactions. Part of this evolution comes as your own interests and posting change to reflect the changing nature of the environment in which you work. And part of this evolution occurs as you continue to find the keywords, in other words, the jargon, that define the sense of community that draws you and your colleagues together through day-to-day exchanges, planning, and actions designed to foster positive change in your world.

Your straightforward use of tags on WordPress can help readers quickly locate content on your blog if you use the part of the platform that produces a tag cloud—a visual representation of the tags/terms you most consistently use in your writing. The more often you use a tag, the larger it appears in the tag cloud that is incorporated into your blog site. (Because my blog and my work focus on training, learning, community, and collaboration, those words are among the largest in my own tag cloud that appears in a column on the right-hand side of that site.) You can further help your readers quickly find content by using a "Categories" widget on WordPress or a "Labels" widget on Blogger. Terms appearing within those displays provide readers with a quick introduction to the general themes you are pursuing, indicate the number of posts on your blog that address those themes, and lead readers to those articles if they click on the category or label of interest to them. The categories and labels, furthermore, can help you lead readers to those posts even if they are not on your blog site: by copying the URL that each category or label has, you can share that URL via other social media platforms or email to provide quick access to topics that may be of interest to those with whom you are working or attempting to cultivate as supporters or collaborators.

—ฅฅฅ—

SETTING UP YOUR BLOG

There are numerous wonderful websites, online documents—including the PCDN (Peace and Collaborative Development Network) "Blogging for Social Change & Impact" guide[8]—and books that can guide you through the myriad details of setting up, writing for, and maintaining a blog. They address topics including your choice of a platform (e.g., WordPress, Blogger, and Tumblr; please see the "Choosing a Platform" section of this chapter for a brief introduction to that topic); the steps you will take to make your content more easily found within the blog itself as well as through Internet searches (please see the "On Tagging Content" Spotlight in this chapter); guides on how to write nonfiction or, more specifically, articles for your blog; and suggestions for preparing your text before it is posted on your blog.

An often-overlooked question to be resolved is whether to compose the text of your blog posts within the platform itself—which has become consistently easier to do over the years as the platforms include increasingly sophisticated word-processing capabilities—or to compose it within a word-processing program with which you are familiar and then transfer the text into the blogging platform. My own preference—after unexpectedly losing nearly completed drafts within WordPress when my computer froze up—is to use my word-processing software, save drafts-in-process frequently (as I do with all writing-in-progress), and retain those word-processed documents within that software and on a flash drive so I can avoid the painful and frustrating experience of trying to re-create something I had struggled to polish before it disappeared. I often find myself fine-tuning the text even after I have transferred it into WordPress but before I post it for public consumption, so I take the extra time required to carry those final edits back into the word-processed document to be sure I have adequate backups for content I do not want to lose.

A particularly interesting part of blogging is that it can function at several levels: as an ongoing series of stand-alone pieces that remain available as long as the blog remains online; as interrelated pieces that include links to previous pieces to create an ongoing resource; and as part of an overall evolving body of work that can be quoted, used, and adapted by you as well as by others who are attracted to your work. You can expedite that process of adaptation and sharing by choosing a Creative Commons license that encourages use of your work along with whatever level of attribution you request through your choice of a license.

CHOOSING A PLATFORM

Among the most popular blogging platforms are WordPress, Blogger, Medium, and Tumblr, and there are certainly plenty more, as summarized in *wpbeginner's* "How to Choose the Best Blogging Platform in 2020 (Compared)" blog post.[9] Each provides a free, robust forum that allows you to compose text within that platform or prepare text in a word-processing program where you can edit your text and embed hyperlinks to related material before saving that original version, then cutting and pasting the completed text into the blog site. Each allows you to combine words, photographs, and videos seamlessly and engagingly to more fully tell your story. Each offers the possibility of providing readers with text that can be skimmed or more fully read start to finish or in a more rewarding and time-consuming way—by following links to other resources that more richly explore the themes you have developed into your own blog post. And each provides opportunities for engagement through expanded online conversations that often cannot be anticipated at the time you prepare and post your original contribution on your blog.

Because there are many similarities between what the Google-owned Blogger platform and the free version of WordPress offer, the choice between the two is substantially one of personal preference. In setting up my own blog in June 2009, I opted for WordPress because it was what other writers I knew were using; Jill Hurst-Wahl, in choosing Blogger for her *Digitization 101* blog,[10] was guided in a similar way: "It was there."[11] Samantha Adams Becker chose Tumblr "so I could easily and instantly publish my blog post and for the potential of community"—but is considering switching to a different platform because Tumblr, to her, is "feeling a little outdated."[12]

I have, after a decade of using WordPress, come to appreciate the flexibility it offers not only in terms of posting content but, more importantly, the various unanticipated possibilities I continue to explore—not the least of which is to use it as a secondary website by setting up a variety of tabs at the top of the site itself (the "Home" page, which has the blog content; an "About" page, which allows me to provide readers with background about what I am doing and exploring; a "Presentations/Courses" page that provides numerous examples of my work in lifelong learning; a "Publications" page that provides links to published articles and books; a "Recommended Associates" page to highlight the work of those with whom I collaborate; and "Testimonials" to provide references for those interested in seeing how my work has been received). I also use WordPress as a secondary website for the Hidden Garden Steps project,[13] and I occasionally contribute to the *T Is for Training* blog on WordPress.[14]

—⚬⚬⚬—

On a Blogger's Code of Conduct

Reacting to harassment directed toward a fellow blogger in 2007, O'Reilly Media Founder Tim O'Reilly briefly proposed a "Blogger's

Code of Conduct"—which immediately became a much-targeted and criticized proposal among those who saw it as a form of censorship. Summarized at the end of Wikipedia's "Blog" article,[15] the seven recommendations included ignoring trolls; telling people who were behaving badly that they were, in fact, behaving badly; and not saying anything online that you wouldn't say face-to-face. It was the first line, however, that seems to have caused the most emotional reactions: taking responsibility for comments posted on your blog as well as for the content you post. Subjected to intense criticism, O'Reilly withdrew the proposal a week later,[16] but the summary remains available on Wikipedia and the initial draft is accessible on O'Reilly's blog.[17]

Other similar online documents offering guidance as you consider how to approach your own blogging include the "Code of Ethics for Bloggers, Social Media and Content Creators"[18] posted by Morten Rand-Hendriksen, an instructor, educator, and speaker at LinkedIn Learning. The Bloggers' Code of Ethics—attributed to CyberJournalist.net[19]—is more detailed than the proposal initially advanced by O'Reilly. It has numerous suggestions grouped together under three main points: "Be Honest and Fair"; "Minimize Harm"; and "Be Accountable." Rand-Hendriksen's proposal is even more detailed, with a short version and a long version exploring a variety of issues and situations. The long version begins with "the role of the bloggers and online content creators in society" and continues with sections on "integrity and responsibility," "content creator conduct and relations with the sources," and "publication rules."

Familiarizing yourself with these documents will help you anticipate some of the challenges you will face as a blogger and, more importantly, avoid those problems in the first place.

—⟁⟁⟁—

Tumblr takes a different approach. Whereas WordPress and Blogger start with text as the assumed central feature and allow you to insert images and links to a variety of resources, Tumblr's format begins with your choice as to whether you are going to feature text, a photo, a quote, a link to another resource, or a video, and it includes options for featuring chats or audio materials. Tumblr's templates then allow you to easily build your post around whatever element you have chosen to be highlighted at the top of the post. As is the case with many social media tools and platforms, Tumblr appears to have been designed with enough flexibility to provide creative users with a variety of options. Created as a platform for short posts, it has nothing that prevents you from creating posts as long (or as short) as any that you will find on WordPress or Blogger. Samantha Adams Becker has consistently used it for her full-length *Hey Kid* blog posts,[20] and former president Barack Obama was among those who used it (through a Barack Obama for President account and the Organizing for Action account[21]) for political and social-activism purposes. A quick search within Tumblr itself shows that numerous organizations (e.g., the ACLU, Doctors Without Borders, Greenpeace, #MarchForOurLives: Los Angeles, Planned Parenthood, the Sierra Club, and the Transgender Law Center) actively maintain a presence on Tumblr.

A broader online search conducted with Google, however, highlights a problem you face if you want your content easily found: using the search terms "[organization name] blog" (e.g., "ACLU blog") tends to lead you to the organization's main blog rather than making you aware that the organization has a presence on Tumblr. What this suggests is that Tumblr is not the place to be if you're trying to be readily and highly visible to those who may be interested in you, but it's an option to consider if you determine that current and prospective members of your community are using Tumblr. As with all social media tools, Tumblr can work well for you if that's where your audience is, but it can be a waste of time if your current and prospective audience is elsewhere.

THE CONVERSATIONAL NATURE OF BLOGS

If you are looking for immediate, abundant, consistent forms of interaction with your supporters, blogging may initially be very disappointing to you. Only the most engaged among your readers will take the time to interact with you by commenting on your blog—which can feel very discouraging if you fall into the trap of checking for responses every five minutes after posting a piece that you absolutely adored and were sure was going to immediately change the world. Colleagues who can see that thousands of people are visiting their sites to read their posts often see little more than a handful of posted responses—and then generally only when they are addressing the timeliest or most controversial of issues. The long-term impacts of their (and your) work, however, become clear as that work is integrated into their (and your) other activities through social media platforms.

In the best of all worlds, the blogging you produce will elicit positive, action-based responses that bring you and members of your community closer to the goals you have set for yourselves in terms of contributing to positive change. This can include readers using their own social media accounts to comment on and post links to what you have written so that your message reaches a wider audience. It can also include those all-too-rare but very encouraging responses posted on your blog. And in an extremely satisfying way, your blog posts can initiate conversations that continue in the form of other bloggers' acknowledgment of and response to your work in their own blogs—which is something I saw within #etmooc (Educational Technology & Media massive open online course) in 2013 when that global learning community comprised of approximately 1,500 learners-as-activists were reading one another's work through a central online site where all participants' blog posts were collected and readily available for review.

One of the most unexpected, pleasurable, and productive examples I saw came when a few of us were exploring the ways that asynchronous postings from a variety of learners were creating what was, to us, a new form of communication—conversations made up of moments that extended for weeks and, in some cases, months (explored throughout this book, particularly in the "Elements of Social Media" section of chapter 1). It was a simple and wonderful process. It began when one course participant, in a blog post directed toward others in #etmooc but available to anyone who came across her blog, mentioned and provided a link to a readily available research paper that introduced the concept of those asynchronous online conversations. The paper, by Pekka Ihanainen and John Moravec,[22] remained open to modifications at any time by those willing to enter the conversation, and was an example of the concept it was exploring. My classmate's initial post caught my attention, led me to read and reread that complex paper, and inspired me to write my own blog post that extended the conversational moment she had initiated.[23] This, of course, drew in others within the course and created a few other interrelated posts that not only carried the conversation further within the #etmooc community, but introduced people within our own (non-#etmooc) communities of learning to the concept.

We will never know how far that concept traveled, nor will we know how many people have begun incorporating those extended-moment asynchronous conversations into their own training-teaching-learning efforts as a result of having read, responded to, and sought opportunities to modify their own approach to working with learners by adapting this style of conversation. It is, however, safe to say that those of us who experimented with the technique through blogging continue to create new opportunities for making learning more engaging, memorable, and actionable than it otherwise might be. And you can play equally important behind-the-scenes roles in promoting positive change within your communities through blogging if you decide to pursue it.

—*⟨•⟩⟨•⟩⟨•⟩*—

When Your Needs and Interests Change

No blog has to remain static or last forever. If your interests are changing, you can shift the focus of your blog to keep up with those changes. You can expect to see longtime readers fall away if your interests and the causes you are supporting are becoming different than theirs. You might, on the other hand, see your most loyal readers stay with you as you also attract new readers and community partners who are drawn to what you are now addressing.

If you do decide that the blog you have been maintaining is no longer worth nurturing, you can follow the example set by *Library Journal* "2011 Mover and Shaker" Buffy Hamilton, who maintained her *The Unquiet Librarian* blog[24] for a decade before creating an entirely new blog (*Living in the Layers*[25]). The writing on *The Unquiet Librarian* was consistently an engaging mixture of advocacy for and observations about innovations in librarianship, and Hamilton consistently drew readers into the changing positions she held in a variety of school libraries. When she finally made a break with librarianship to return, full-time, to teaching, she wrote a final column to explain to *Unquiet Librarian* readers why she was leaving that blog behind. She also included an invitation to join her on the new blog as she chronicles her explorations as a language arts instructor promoting literacy through innovative interactions with her learners. The content of *The Unquiet Librarian* remains accessible and, in some ways, interwoven with the content on her new blog because, in an essential way, both focus on building communities with learners in learning organizations. By leaving the earlier content intact, she also keeps a door open to adding new content to *The Unquiet Librarian* if her ever-evolving interests take her back into that wonderful intersection of advocacy, learning, schools, and libraries.

———⁓⁓⁓———

Not all comments made about your blog are going to be positive—but that, in itself, can produce positive results. Jill Hurst-Wahl recalls one such instance:

> I once wrote a blog post that angered someone *and* also started a larger technical conversation. I oopsed in saying that "X" had written about something and that he was wrong. Well, he wrote to defend his thought process, and that started a conversation that was really interesting. While I didn't understand the technicalities, it was nice to know that I had started it!
>
> People will walk up [at conferences] and say, "I know you." It is scary and thrilling at the same time, and it has happened in odd places, and even with people who are not from the US. It means that I have placed myself into a larger conversation about libraries/digitization/copyright which people acknowledge and respect. In some ways, it has made me more mindful of my audience.[26]

This potential for interactions does raise an important issue for you to consider as you set up and maintain your blog: how much control you want to maintain over what appears there—particularly when content posted by readers becomes uncivil or worse (a topic explored more fully in the "On a Blogger's Code of Conduct" Spotlight in this chapter and in chapter 10, "Facing Incivility: Trolls, Online Harassment, and Fake News"). Some bloggers maintain completely open access, allowing anyone to comment on posts. Others use the options within their blogging platform to completely disable any comments at all—an approach that becomes particularly appealing after they have been subjected to threats, harassment, or less alarming forms of incivility. The approach I have taken and highly recommend is to allow comments that you must first approve through a simple process of moderation; this helps establish the tenor and quality of the discourse taking place so that others

interested in contributing positively to the conversation feel encouraged—and safe enough—to do so.

—⟨⟨⟩⟩—

Pro Tips: Blogging for Social Change

"A blog for an individual or organization should be both an information
source and a personal space for ideas, thoughts and reflection—also a
place to workshop wild and crazy and odd ideas."—Maurice Coleman,
whose *T Is for Training* blog (managed by Jill Hurst-Wahl) primarily
serves as a place for notes about and resources to augment his *T Is for
Training* podcasts

"Push your posts out into the world. In other words, use social media
and other tools to disseminate your posts and get them noticed. Yes,
you need to market your blog."—Jill Hurst-Wahl, who writes for her
own *Digitization 101* blog and manages the *T Is for Training* blog

"Be consistent, and consistently post new content. People will expect
that. If you are consistent, and churning out new content, you'll continue to gain readers and followers. That's assuming your content is actually good and useful."—David Lee King, who writes about tech trends—
and much more—on his *David Lee King* blog

—⟨⟨⟩⟩—

Moderating content on my blog is fairly easy. The settings within Word-
Press provide automatic notification via email whenever someone I
have not previously encountered attempts to post a comment. Those
whose comments have previously been approved can post directly, by-
passing that level of moderation, and I still retain the ability to delete
any content that I see as beneath the quality of the conversation I am
trying to foster. If a comment from a first-time contributor is relevant to
what I have posted, I simply accept the comment by using the dashboard WordPress provides, and it instantly appears for other readers to
see so they can respond if they want to join the conversation. If the
comment is something that is clearly an act of trolling or any other form
of harassment, I can delete it by choosing the option to send it to the
trash function within WordPress rather than allowing it to appear on
the blog.

There is a separate type of comment that requires a bit more thought, but becomes easy to deal with as you become more experienced at spotting it: those comments from spammers or bots. They initially appear to be neutral—sometimes congratulatory—responses, but don't directly address the content of the post. They sometimes even seem to be responding to something else entirely, hinting that they had been generated by an algorithm programmed to pull key words out of your original post but not quite sophisticated enough to sound like anything other than a third-rate version of Google Translate. It's fairly easy, within the set-up of the WordPress dashboard, to go to the site from which the comment was ostensibly generated; this gives you an opportunity to learn more about the person posting the comment—or to determine that it is simply an automated response meant to draw others to a website that has nothing to do with what you are discussing. Those sites, in my experience, have ranged from websites selling products to Russian-language sites offering opportunities to engage in online gambling—and it takes little time for me to remove them from my account before they actually appear on the blog for public consumption.

NEXT STEPS

To gain a better understanding of how blogging can produce positive opportunities and results for you and those you serve, please try either of the following exercises involving a step you are taking to promote a small- or large-scale change in a community with which you work:

- Create a blog post that is designed to be shared and/or elicit responses or actions from those who see it. Respond, within the platform you have chosen, to any responses you receive to your initial post.
- Go to the ChangeTheWorld-Co community on Slack; initiate or join a discussion on that site in the channel designated for chapter 6; and respond to at least two of the responses your post inspires. (If you have not already joined that community, you can do so by contacting me directly at paul@paulsignorelli.com and including a brief—one-line—description of your interest in learning more about using social media to change the world.)

7

BROADCASTS AND PODCASTS

YouTube, TalkShoe, and Zencastr

Incorporating videos and podcasts into your work can be far simpler than you initially imagine and can open up new forms of expression for you to use in engaging your current and prospective partners in fostering positive social change. This chapter explores how activists are incorporating YouTube and podcasting platforms into their change-the-world tool kit.

If the thought of reaching your current or prospective community of activists and other collaborators via YouTube or podcasts feels daunting, start simply, openly, and honestly—with something you know—as Phillip "Brail" Watson does. Watson, on his Facebook "Our Story" page, describes himself as "a classically trained vocalist, cellist, songwriter, rapper, clinician, producer and Berklee College of Music graduate" who wants to "change the world through music."[1] His extensive, well-developed, engaging presence on YouTube, Facebook, Twitter, and other social media platforms fully integrates his commitment to music, spirituality, and social change in ways that make it seem like the easiest thing in the world to do. And it can be for you, too, if you pursue it as diligently and purposefully as he does.

If you spend time with Watson online by exploring his use of social media, you begin to see and appreciate the possibilities available through the effective use of a platform like YouTube. His stunningly moving TEDxTopeka talk "Giving Back"[2] begins with a brief, beautiful, sung prayer—obviously an element of his work that flows from the core of all he is. He then quickly pulls you in by admitting "I'm going to do this all wrong"—an admission that challenges and begs you to stay with him to see where he is going in the eighteen minutes he has under the standard TED (Technology, Entertainment, Design) talk format. He asks you—just as he asks the live audience he is addressing in that recorded talk—to walk with him, to see what he sees from his perspective, and to "feel the places" where he has been in the hope that you will come to understand, as he has, the value of giving something back to the community you cherish. It's an invitation to be part of something positive, something greater than you already are or might ever be—and it is an effective call to action because Watson draws upon his highly developed use of language, poetry, musicianship, and inspirational skills to integrate all of those elements into the wonderfully moving video that documents his TEDxTopeka talk in 2015.

This is about far more than making and placing content on a social media site; it is about using everything you have developed and will continue to develop to effectively reach audiences and inspire positive action. It is about developing a body of work that weaves through everything else you do. It is about integrating that work in unexpectedly creative ways with other work you do and other opportunities you pursue. It is about transforming the (sometimes) simple act of recording and sharing your thoughts on YouTube and through podcasts into an act of inviting engagement with people you may never actually meet. It is about recognizing that you don't have to physically meet someone to be drawn into their causes and inspired to action by them—or inspire them and draw them into yours.

Describing the unexpected sequence of events that led to me finding and being inspired by Watson provides some lessons worth learning:

- Although you want to have a specific audience in mind as you prepare a YouTube video or podcast, you will have no idea initially of how broad and diverse an audience you will eventually reach and inspire.
- A presentation given in one venue, e.g., the TEDxTopeka talk, that is recorded, posted, and shared online, gains an extended life far beyond anything you could have provided if you had simply given that presentation and then moved on to something else.

- The efforts you make to reach your audience produce only a small part of what is accomplished when others see and share your work; those efforts offer the same expansion you see when others retweet your tweets or share your Facebook posts in ways that produce rhizomatic expansion[3] of what you thought might be little more than a moment lived and then forgotten.

My initial unplanned step toward finding Watson online was taken when my Topeka-based colleague David Lee King and I were doing our interview for this chapter. I had asked David for examples he had seen of how YouTube was part of the process of promoting positive change within a community. He did not mention Watson; instead, he responded with a description of a magnificent activist's-dream initiative, Go Topeka's Momentum 2022, which is described on the project's website as "a comprehensive, actionable, and consensus-based community plan to guide the Topeka-Shawnee Counties collective actions in the years to come."[4] King pointed me toward a two-minute video that very much impressed me: "Topeka & Shawnee County Have Momentum," posted on YouTube by the citizen-activists in the Greater Topeka Partnership.[5] It seemed to have everything that a video call-to-action should have: high production values, a clear message (that Topeka has lots to offer and can become even better if community partners work together to build upon its existing strengths to chip away at its weaknesses), and an obvious call to action—until I heard from Jill Hurst-Wahl during our conversations for this chapter.

There is no gentle way to express what Jill noted after viewing the video I had so enthusiastically shared: it didn't have many images of people, but the images included in the video did little to hint that nearly 25 percent of Topeka's population is African American or Hispanic. That's when Jill found and offered a different video version of the topic: Watson's "Topeka Proud" video, posted on Vimeo.[6] Same city, much different viewpoint—and one that aligns with parts of the Momentum 2022 initiative calling for efforts to foster and promote greater diversity and inclusivity in Topeka. And seeing what Watson had produced led me to seek out much more of what he was doing—on YouTube, Facebook, Twitter, and elsewhere.

This provides another opportunity for a reminder worth repeating: you can certainly choose one specific social media platform that best suits your goals as someone attempting to foster positive change in your community, but creating an integrated presence over multiple platforms tremendously increases the chances that you will reach the largest possible group of community partners to help you reach those goals.

As you move into a more complete exploration of YouTube and podcasts as tools you can use in your efforts, it's worth noting that there is at least one more encouraging piece to the Go Topeka/Topeka Proud story: a second video, posted on YouTube by the Greater Topeka Partnership eight months after the first one appeared. This video pushes the story forward with a much broader cast of characters featuring obvious ethnic diversity through the inclusion of Enimini Ekong (Brown v. Board of Education National Historical Site), Leo Espinoza (College and Career Advocate, Topeka USD 501 Schools), Marcus Clark (senior pastor, Love Fellowship Church, East Topeka), Angel Zimmerman (Zimmerman & Zimmerman, PA), and others.[7] This is clearly a community that is effectively and creatively working to promote the most positive results it can imagine.

The remainder of this chapter explores some of the ways you can more effectively reach members of your community through YouTube and podcasting.

INTRODUCTION TO YOUTUBE

To begin understanding how to approach YouTube to promote positive social change, you can turn to YouTube itself—starting with the YouTube Creator Academy video "Inspiring Social Change on Your [YouTube] Channel,"[8] produced in collaboration with Creators for Change fellows Leena Normington (*Leena Norms* YouTube channel featuring videos on feminism, politics, and other topics); Subhi Taha (*subhitaha* channel featuring discussions regarding how being a Muslim-American has shaped his identity); and Niharika Nm (*niharikanm* channel featuring videos designed to inspire young viewers to shape their world). It's a perfect example of how the platform itself is a magnificent training-teaching-learning resource that demonstrates the power of visual storytelling in helping you and others foster change within the communities you serve. (For more about YouTube channels, please see the Spotlight section "On YouTube Channels" in this chapter.)

The summary at the end of this well-produced, easy-to-assimilate overview gives you basic, encouraging, positive guidance:

"Find a topic you're passionate about"—something you probably did long before you decided to read this book.

"Start a conversation"—something which, by now, should be increasingly comfortable for you through whatever you have begun or continued doing by effectively integrating your use of Facebook, Twitter, Instagram, or any other social media tool with which you have become comfortable as part of your overall social-change tool kit.

"Engage with others who identify with you"—a natural extension of the process of exploring the *social* aspects of social media rather than seeing social media platforms as simply another way to engage in one-way broadcasting of the messages you are attempting to convey.

"Help people see other perspectives"—a goal toward which you move, incrementally, every time you positively, engagingly tell your story, or part of your story, through your use of the social media tools you are exploring.

"Create positive social change"—a process you are continuing to master through your own efforts and the support you find among those with whom you interact face-to-face, online, and in blended (onsite-online) settings.

Just as I learned about Brail Watson's commitment to promoting social change in Topeka and elsewhere through music by exploring content he had posted in a variety of settings, you can learn more about what YouTube can do for you—and the causes you are promoting—by exploring those YouTube Creators for Change fellows' channels.

———⚬⚬⚬———

On YouTube Channels

YouTube channels parallel the concept of traditional broadcast and cable channels in the sense that they provide an outlet for disseminating content under some sort of branded identity—your name, your company name, or any other name that identifies the channel in a way that helps you reach your audience. They obviously do not, however, carry the heavy investment costs that accompany the start-up of broadcast and cable outlets. All you need is a Google account, a few minutes to create the channel through YouTube, and an idea of how you will use that channel to reach and interact with the audience you are attempting to engage.

A personal or business YouTube account allows you to post content you have created and, through creation of playlists, content produced and posted by others. You can also use that channel to interact with others through YouTube Community posts and livestreaming content to more fully engage your current and potential collaborators.

The fifty most popular channels center around entertainment, comedy, and sports videos. They represent the creative efforts of a global network comprised of people from more than forty different countries, and have anywhere from twenty to more than seventy million subscribers.[9] Your own efforts, of course, can be much more modest in terms of the number of people you initially want to reach and the way in which you approach the nurturing of your channel. A *Social Media Examiner* article published in 2018 offers "15 Tips for Growing Your YouTube Channel," including developing "a sustainable video production workflow," replicating "topics or tactics from top-performing videos," and collaborating with others—a natural step for anyone building a coalition to foster positive social change.[10]

"I think the way YouTube allows users to create their own channels is important," Samantha Adams Becker observes. "It's very easy to connect all of a producer's videos, watch them in an intentional order, and even get recommendations on the side for similar or related videos they might enjoy based on the current video/channel. I also think the ability to subscribe to a channel and be notified when a new video is added is important. All a producer has to do is upload and publish a video, and suddenly an entire community of subscribers know about it with no direct communication from the producer—which is a great concept for mobilizing people pretty quickly."[11]

For instructions on how to establish your own channel, please visit the YouTube "Create a New Channel" page at https://support .google.com/youtube/answer/1646861?hl=en.[12]

If you start with Normington's *Leena Norms* channel, you find a TED Talk–length (eighteen-minute) rumination and call to action on the theme she calls "Go Back to Where You Came From,"[13] posted in 2017. It serves as a wonderful example of what a twenty-first-century lecture can be—something far more expansive, creative, and compelling than many of the I-speak-You-listen-We-all-fall-asleep presentations that have made many people ask whether The Lecture Is Dead. (For the record, I don't at all believe the lecture is dead; I believe it is continuing to evolve in ways that incorporate technology into lectures in ways previously unimagined and in ways we still cannot even begin to fully imagine in a world where technology is evolving rapidly.) "Go Back to Where You Came From" is a relatively high-end production that suggests plenty of experience with video-editing tools, the use of imagery (i.e., still photographs, manipulated graphics, and video) integrated with the spoken word, and visual and audio juxtapositions that themselves push the narrative forward without explicitly being stated through lecture-as-words. Sometimes, she directly addresses you with an intimacy that suggests face-to-face contact, or she includes background narration while imagery propels the narrative forward. Consistently, she displays a masterful ability to use the YouTube platform to interweave a video into the online text descriptions and call to action that are attached to the video on YouTube—including a list of action points to be taken by those moved by what Normington presents. Her text on the site also provides a list of further resources to be perused by those wanting to know more about the topic she addresses (e.g., what it means to be British—or, by extension, a citizen in any part of a world where immigration remains a potential conduit to citizenship). Most importantly, she inspires viewers to pursue those all-important opportunities for interactions—positive as well as negative—among those who have been moved by this contemporary online lecture that continues to have a life and an opportunity to foster positive change as long as it remains available online.

Subhi Taha's *subhitaha* channel offers a varied compendium of reflections on growing up as a Muslim in the United States after 9/11. There are reflections on his experiences seeking work, his response to the Muslim community's use of social media, and his personal reactions to a variety of other topics drawn from his own passions. His "Just Say It" video, posted September 25, 2017, appears to be one of his most polished efforts to date.[14] Taha avoids much of the direct face-to-face approach you see in Normington's "Go Back to Where You Came From"—yet he is no less effective in addressing viewers to foster the positive change he is seeking. Taha relies on strong, beautifully composed narration spoken behind a series of images drawn from news clips, videos of himself, and simple, moving special effects to help convey his belief that refusing to speak out in the face of social injustice makes him—and everyone else—complicit in those injustices. He leaves you understanding the importance of deciding to "just say it" instead of standing silently by as if your voice cannot be a catalyst for change—and he makes you, too, want to join him in saying it through your work on YouTube and other social media platforms.

Moving over to Niharika Nm's *niharikanm* channel provides an entirely different approach to a much different challenge: combatting the hateful impact of cyberbullying by online trolls—a topic more fully explored in chapter 10 of this book. Nm, in her ten-minute "You're Ugly"[15] Creators for Change video, initially gently lures you into her topic—and her world—with playful images drawn from her daily life. It only takes a couple of minutes, however, for you to begin understanding—and, more importantly, empathizing with—the emotionally crippling pain she feels as anonymous hate messages making fun of her appearance begin reaching her through her mobile phone. This is first conveyed through the embedding of some of those messages into the video as she describes the cumulative impact they are having on her—draining her enthusiasm for life, making her want to change her appearance. The impact becomes even more profound when one of those hateful screeds creatively and unexpectedly appears as a hate message scrawled across her mirror as she is applying makeup in response to her growing belief that her physical appearance is somehow responsible for the abuse. A variety of other editing effects carry you further into her world as she reaches an emotional breaking point—and the video clearly becomes an online poem that carries you through her own recovery from the online abuse. In the same way that Watson uses music to foster social change and Normington uses the potential of video to demonstrate how lectures are being transformed through contemporary technology, Nm shows you how poetry continues to evolve through the use of technology available to you. The ultimate impact of watching that emotionally wrenching online video poem/call to action is to remind you that you have, at your core, a sense of the poetry of your own life and the issues you are attempting to address—and a sense that, in your own way, in your own unique voice, you, too, can use YouTube and other social media platforms to help create the world you want to inhabit.

Although the examples cited up to this point demonstrate a great deal of sophistication in terms of how video can be used to promote your efforts, you don't have to gain that much experience before developing and posting your own videos, as Samantha Adams Becker suggests.

> Anyone with a smartphone instantly has a video production studio in their pocket. There are so many apps that enable users to take their videos to the next level, adding music, overlaying graphics, editing on-the-go, and immediately uploading and publishing the content to YouTube. Plus, YouTube generates very sharable short links that make it easier for the user and any viewers to embed the videos on other social media platforms and even on their professional or personal website. It's not just about the video as a product but the shareability of it. Producers can choose which frame from the video becomes the "thumbnail" or the image that represents the video, selecting one that is eye-catching and impactful.[16]

Some organizations are tremendously adept at integrating their YouTube offerings with other social media posts, Jill Hurst-Wahl notes:

> I really like how the Poor People's Campaign: A National Call for a Moral Revival is using video—livestream, YouTube, Facebook. They have live-streamed their events, then archived them for later viewing. They took their New Year's Eve Watch Night event, streamed it, rebroadcasted it, and then divided it into three audio podcasts! They are trying to rally people and educate people, so the videos are important. [Their] video [please see "This Wall Is Sin!" in the "Five YouTube Social Change Videos Worth Watching" Spotlight section of this chapter] really demonstrates to me the power of video. Part of it is people wading out into the Rio Grande so that immigrants can talk to their Mexican family members. The video is a shorter piece created from the event they did that day in Texas. . . . There is a point where you can see people on the other side of the wall and conversations happening.[17]

For a much deeper dive into using YouTube, please visit the YouTube Creators Academy site, which offers numerous free, self-directed online courses designed to help you create, use, and manage a YouTube channel: https://creatoracademy.youtube.com/page/education. [18]

For more than fifty examples of videos designed to foster social change, please visit the YouTube Creators for Change "50+ Films That Bring Us Together" page: https://www.youtube.com/channel/UCYJJpu7FLQqu788cusj6nIg. [19]

———❧❧❧———

Five YouTube Social Change Videos Worth Watching

"Highlights: The Evolution of a Social Activist (How I Found My Voice!)" https://www.youtube.com/watch?v=wI69NYOo5uM [20]

"Interview with the Founders of Black Lives Matter: Alicia Garza, Patrisse Cullors, Opal Tometi" https://www.youtube.com/watch?v=tbicAmaXYtM [21]

"Kid President Asks 'What Makes an Awesome Leader?'" https://www.youtube.com/watch?v=KdL4o7wU0CQ [22]

"Social Media: Online Activism" https://www.youtube.com/watch?v=AN-kIJI_5wg [23]

"This Wall Is Sin!" https://www.youtube.com/watch?v=A7bJjMH5oPc [24]

———❧❧❧———

INTRODUCTION TO PODCASTING

In the same way that creating and posting content on YouTube can help you engage with current and potential collaborators, podcasting can create synchronous as well as asynchronous connections that contribute to the development of positive, extended, potentially global communities of action.

Among those whose work you have already seen in other social media channels and who actively reach members through their audience are DeRay Mckesson. His *Pod Save the People*,[25] which began recording in April 2017, explores news, culture, social justice, and politics through a combination of interviews and reports on news stories that might not otherwise receive much attention. His earliest episodes included interviews with US Senator Cory Booker and Edward Snowden. Topics explored with *Pod Save the People* regulars Brittany Packnett, Sam Sinyangwe, and Clint Smith have ranged from healthcare legislation and the opioid crisis to #MeToo, #DACA, and voter suppression.

Others whose work you have encountered in this book foster social change through interviews they provide via podcasting rather than creating and managing their own podcasts. Executive Director of 18 Million Rising Cayden Mak, for example, discussed his life and work in Episode 91 of *Model MAJORITY Podcast*.[26] Canadian activist-author-speaker Hannah Alper has also appeared in podcasts, including Jennifer Hill's *Get Yourself the Job* podcast, to discuss her work and her book, *Momentus: Small Acts, Big Change*.[27]

Two change-oriented podcast communities with which I remain involved are Maurice Coleman's *T Is for Training* and Jonathan Nalder's *Edunauts*. Both are nurtured in ways designed to stimulate positive social change through better training-teaching-learning efforts. Both follow complementary paths to engagement without being identical in their approach. *T Is for Training* is open to anyone who wants to participate in the biweekly recording sessions exploring developments, trends, and challenges for library staff and users, while *Edunauts* focuses on the FutureWe future literacies framework designed to help learners and leaders, worldwide, develop skills that will be useful in contemporary workplaces; the podcast generally has a limited number of preselected panelists engaged in the biweekly conversations. Neither *T Is for Training* nor *Edunauts* requires tremendous expenditures to maintain; they are activist-driven, community-supported efforts where the dedication of a continually evolving set of participants provides what is needed to nurture and sustain them. Most importantly, both demonstrate that a podcast can be far more than a recording that is passively consumed without producing concrete results: the podcasts are regularly scheduled gatherings of their sometimes-overlapping communities that function effectively online as well as onsite when members of those communities meet face-to-face at conferences, workshops, and other meetings where their shared interests draw them together.

"I wanted to replicate the vibe and comradery I felt at conferences where I was surrounded with brilliant members of my 'tribe' of trainers, computer folks and other gear/nerd/cool folk heads," Coleman says in recalling his motivation for starting *T Is for Training*. "I wanted that all of the time—not just a couple of times of the year if I was lucky, so, I took from a friend's podcast and said, 'Why not me?' That was 2008, and we have been going strong ever since. . . . I was also lucky to have the support of my library—and, specifically, my boss and director at the time—to do this during work hours. We believe in professional development, and my podcast continues to be a great source of my professional development [although no longer produced during work hours]."[28]

⸺◈◈◈⸺

Pro Tips: YouTube

"Including closed captioning is vital. YouTube videos are widely shared across Facebook, Twitter, and other social media platforms so that people can watch them directly from their feeds without ever leaving where they are. People often have their phone and computer volumes turned low or muted, so when the video starts automatically playing in their feed, it will be less effective without sound. Integrating captions means that people in quiet spaces can digest the content easily."—Samantha Adams Becker, consultant, whose social media posts have fostered growth within online communities

"Learn by doing. Do it often. Give your videos good descriptions. Include any relevant hashtags. Caption the videos. Organize your videos. Push the videos out using all of your social media tools. Figure out what you need to do to improve the quality, but don't strive for perfection. Social change is not reliant on perfection!"—Jill Hurst-Wahl, whose work has facilitated productive engagement among members of nonprofit organizations she has joined and served

"There are some YouTube best practices to put into practice—things like starting with your most important content right at the beginning—no fade-ins, credits, or sappy music. Making sure to have a next step—after watching the video, what do you want me to do? Include that in the video! Keeping it short, being consistent, i.e., one video a week/month, and stick to that for a year. Sharing the video everywhere—your website/blog, in social media, etc. Also, posting it separately on Facebook—because, for some odd reason, Facebook favors Facebook-native video over YouTube video."—David Lee King, whose work on social media is well-respected within the communities he serves

———⟨⟨⟩⟩———

The mechanical aspects of recording, producing, and making the podcasts accessible via the TalkShoe platform are relatively straightforward. Coleman has a TalkShoe account that provides him and his podcast participants with a dial-in number that can be accessed by phone or via the Internet. As soon as he dials in, the recording automatically begins, and continues until he taps a button that indicates the recording is finished. TalkShoe automatically archives the recording, assigns it a URL, and makes it accessible to anyone interested in listening to it. Coleman works with colleague Jill Hurst-Wahl to promote access to those episodes via social media tools including Twitter, Facebook, and the WordPress blog that Hurst-Wahl maintains as a way of indexing the shows, providing supplementary material, and offering brief summaries of each episode's content. In theory, that blog also offers another opportunity for community engagement through postings on the blog, but that is an option that, so far, has rarely been pursued by *T Is for Training* community members.

Edunauts, with its focus on the FutureWe learning literacies developed by Nalder with tremendous collaboration from his global FutureWe community members, serves to nurture that community, the framework, and the positive changes the framework is designed to support. The podcast, he notes, is an integral part of the overall movement he continues to develop:

> [It is] extremely important for about three reasons. One is the obvious: that producing good content around your mission and sharing it regularly will always help get the word out. But it's also important in that the format means we are discussing and refining the framework and its elements as well as sharing about them, *and* having that regular show means we—and me—as a team are also kept to a schedule and on track, if that makes sense. Oh! I forgot a fourth one: the very fact of having a chat show means inviting guests, which is a process that further develops the network and relationships within it, making the whole community stronger as a result.

The framework that *Edunauts* is set up to unpack and discuss is on paper an "iterative, peer-reviewed" framework, but for that to be true in practice, you have to initiate the discussions and have the forum for it. In this way, creating the podcast has led to changes and updates across the first two literacies—I think two updates to each area so far—so just as the living, live discussions are happening, they are not only for "spreading the word" or promotions, but for refining the group and framework itself. Without the regular short but sharp chats that see the podcast be created, we'd have missed so far about sixteen opportunities to do that refining.[29]

———

Pro Tips: Podcasting

"Be yourself. Be honest. And though it may sound trite, be real. You may have to do some self-promotion in order to reach a larger audience. Also, don't be surprised if your work reaches further than you can imagine."—Maurice Coleman, whose biweekly *T Is for Training* podcast has been reaching community members and other listeners since 2008

"I'm a big proponent of having a format and length in mind for your podcasts. It drives me crazy when someone does a 10-minute podcast one week and a 60-minute podcast the next. I guess I want consistency. And while long podcasts seem to be the thing, keep in mind whether or not you need to go long. There are a few four- to six-minute podcasts that I've listened to that have been quite well done."—Jill Hurst-Wahl, a regular participant on *T Is for Training*

"Have a mix of regular people and guests to provide familiar voices and provide a through-line that keeps things on-theme, while also introducing new ideas and directions. This is a vital blend of structure and surprise that just naturally provides an ongoing energy for the podcast."—Jonathan Nalder, whose biweekly *Edunauts* podcast is part of his effort to help reshape the connection between lifelong learning and the development of workplace skills globally

———

Whereas Coleman serves as his own producer, Nalder relies on Stephen Hurley and his VoicEd network (which uses Zencastr as a platform) to produce and help disseminate the show. Nalder explains this process:

> Getting the technical side right is a huge part of making the show listenable in the first place—without good audio that is promptly mixed and made available, the discussion would never be heard. But the energy it takes to learn and practice it for me/us would have meant the bar was too high to get the chats off the ground—being a volunteer group, it would have at the very least meant it took much longer or didn't last—so, having a partner with that expertise already has set us free to use the volunteer energy we do have just on the discussions.
>
> Stephen, in particular, has a mission that overlaps with especially the community and storytelling aspects of the Future Literacies framework—so, helping us meets his goals and our contributions to his VoicEd community then help that also—but, really, it's just one of those minds-thinking-alike encounters that magnifies what's possible for everyone. In this way, it matches the framework also where no one can really master all the elements in the framework, so it's much better to find partners who complement the skills you do have so you can get busy with the mission itself instead.

NEXT STEPS

To gain a better understanding of how the use of YouTube and podcasting tools can produce positive opportunities and results for you and those you serve, please try either of the following exercises involving a step you are taking to promote a small- or large-scale change in a community with which you work:

- Create a YouTube channel and post a video or playlist, or use equipment available to you to record a short podcast (no more than ten minutes long), that is designed to be shared and/or elicit responses or actions from those who see it; respond, within the social media platform you have chosen, to any responses you receive to your initial post.

- Go to the ChangeTheWorld-Co community on Slack; initiate or join a discussion on that site in the channel designated for chapter 7; and respond to at least two of the responses your post inspires. (If you have not already joined that community, you can do so by contacting me directly at paul@paulsignorelli.com and including a brief—one-line—description of your interest in learning more about using social media to change the world.)

8

VIDEOCONFERENCING AND TELEPRESENCE

Meeting Online to Change the World

Using social media videoconferencing tools can create a sense of physical presence—telepresence—among participants that erases geographic barriers; when used effectively, they create the sense that members of geographically separated communities are working collaboratively, face-to-face, in ways that strengthen community members' ability to meet, plan, and act to change the world using social media. This chapter explores how you can create a sense of telepresence with readily available social media tools.

When members of the Elders Action Network want to meet, they don't immediately begin booking flights, hotel rooms, and meeting sites. They often turn to Zoom, one of several videoconferencing tools that are increasingly becoming low-cost (or no-cost) go-to places for meetings that can combine onsite and online interactions.

The network—primarily comprised of older activists living throughout the United States and actively engaged with one another locally, regionally, nationally, and through international travel and online interactions—includes educators, nonprofit administrators, environmentalists, writers, and others actively working together to change the world. Among the representatives listed on the organization's website and related project sites promoting positive solutions to societal and environmental challenges are Michael Abkin, National Peace Academy board chairman and treasurer;[1] Lynne Iser, founding executive director for the Spiritual Eldering Institute, founder of Elder-Activists-org, a symposium facilitator for the Pachamama Alliance, and a participant in the making of the film *Praying with Lior*, which explores the story of how a member of her family (her stepson) with Down syndrome interacts in his community of faith as he prepares for his bar mitzvah;[2] and Paul Severance, past chair of the coordinating circle for Sage-ing International and congressional liaison for Citizens' Climate Lobby.[3]

Cross-pollination between members of the Elders Action Network and other complementary groups through teleconferencing and other tools is obvious from the most cursory exploration of the network's website. Severance and others are involved in Sage-ing International—another elder organization, dedicated to "teaching/learning, service, and community" in ways that involve mentoring and creating a legacy for its individual members.[4] At least one member is also active in the Seniors Action Network.[5]

Their live and archived Zoom sessions provide a dynamic example of how you can easily use what you already have—a desktop or laptop computer, or a mobile phone or tablet—to incorporate videoconferencing into your work to consistently develop communities committed to fostering positive actions regardless of where you live. Zoom—with free and low-cost versions—offers them a dynamic social media tool that creates an onsite space for workshops, book discussion groups, webinars, and monthly community conversations among members of the organization's "Elder Activists for Social Justice" and "Elders Climate Action" groups. In the live sessions, participants can see any colleague using a webcam and can hear any colleague enabling the audio capabilities of his or her computer or mobile device. Zoom, like many other videoconferencing tools, offers visual options including a screen filled by the image of the person speaking; a screen that has thumbnail images of all participants using their video feed; a space to share material (including slide decks) from a speaker's desktop; and a live chat function that allows for backchannel conversations augmenting what is taking place in the main audio feed.

Some of the community conversation recordings are archived so the life of those meetings/conversations extends far beyond the live events themselves to engage others who are interested in but unavailable to participate live during the recordings.[6] They become part of the seamlessly interwoven conversations you, too, can be having with members of your own community.

As members of the Elders Action Network have discovered, you don't need to be physically present with your colleagues to have "face-to-face" conversations. Using Zoom or other videoconferencing tools can, under the right conditions, make participants feel as if they are in the same space, having productive, community-building interactions regardless of where each participant is physically located. And, as I learned through my experiences with #etmooc, recordings that are well produced can even leave asynchronous participants feeling as if they are/were in the live sessions. (I have repeatedly found myself reaching, without thinking, toward my keyboard to respond to comments in a chat feed before remembering that I am trying to respond to a live conversation that ended days, weeks, or even months earlier.) In many ways, Zoom offers a great contemporary example of how your onsite and online interactions are increasingly merging if you take time to explore how Zoom, Skype, and other videoconferencing tools can create a sense of presence—telepresence or virtual presence—that creates engaging, global spaces where activists work together to foster social change. (Please see "Introduction to Videoconferencing and Telepresence" in this chapter for more on the relationship between videoconferencing and telepresence.) When you explore the possibilities of collaborating online through the use of telepresence tools—those ever-evolving platforms including Skype, Zoom, and Shindig that, when used effectively, can make you feel as if you are in the same room with people who are on the other side of your state, your country, or the world—you discover what so many others before you have realized: your options for communicating with others regardless of your physical locations are continuing to evolve rapidly in ways that can make your work easier than would otherwise be possible.

Exploring the technical side of telepresence tools—which is what this chapter will help you do—provides a somewhat cold, efficient understanding of what they can offer you and those you serve. Actually seeing them used or using them yourself to achieve concrete results carries you right where you need to be: understanding that they can create a sense of presence and engagement that further expands the breadth and depth of your community, your levels of engagement, and the size of the community in which you work, live, and play. (Play, as always, is a key element of using these tools to their fullest potential. Bringing a sense of playfulness to the ways in which you incorporate these tools into your change-the-world efforts is a surefire way to use them to produce results rather than making them the focus of your work and, as a result, detracting from rather than supporting what you and your colleagues are attempting to accomplish.)

INTRODUCTION TO VIDEOCONFERENCING AND TELEPRESENCE

When you consider the differences between teleconferencing,[7] video-conferencing,[8] and telepresence,[9] you are—among other things—usually thinking about the differences between using affordable videoconferencing technology to bring people together for meetings or other conversations (free or low-cost options) and bringing people together through very sophisticated, expensive forms of technology to create a sense that everyone is working together in the same physical space regardless of where in the world they actually are.

Teleconferencing is hardly a new concept; it has been in use for decades through the long-familiar use of telephones and speaker systems in office conference rooms and numerous other settings. The possibilities for productive interactions capable of creating more compelling variations on face-to-face exchanges through teleconferencing expanded and became much more mainstream when live video and audio feeds became available through social media tools including Skype, Google Hangouts, and numerous other low- or no-cost tools. With a bit of planning and practice, users in a variety of settings including businesses, schools, and libraries have found that they can easily create the feeling that participants physically separated by hundreds or thousands of miles can interact as if they are sitting next to each other.

On Developing Your Skills as an Online Presenter-Facilitator

Developing effective, engaging presentation and facilitation skills is, as you probably know, a lifetime endeavor—but this doesn't mean you have to wait a lifetime to dive into settings requiring presentation and facilitation skills. Practice may not make you perfect, but each experience you have presenting information to colleagues, partners, and current or prospective supporters builds upon your previous experiences and, in the best of situations, further hones your skills.

One of the many keys to success is to remember that presenting information and facilitating conversations designed to foster positive change should focus on those with whom you are working—not on you. A common mistake in leading onsite or online sessions is to believe you are the most important person in the physical or virtual room; to the contrary, you can actually be most effective as a facilitator by moving conversations forward toward concrete, positive results—keeping the focus on the goals, not on yourself.

Another key to success is to learn from others. Each time you see another presenter or facilitator in action or watch a TED talk online or participate in a webinar or other online session, you have the opportunity to adapt what appears to be successful for that person and the audience that person is serving. You also can note what does not work for you or other members of that audience and promise yourself you will never do that to a group with which you are working.

A third key to success is to spend time reading books or watching videos produced by those who successfully engage audiences while presenting information or facilitating positive action by focusing on what they hope to accomplish during the time they have with those who turn to them for help. Among the books that might be helpful to you are the following:

Building Online Learning Communities: Effective Strategies for the Virtual Classroom (Second Edition), by Rena Palloff and Keith Pratt (San Francisco: Jossey-Bass, 2007)—A wonderful resource for anyone attempting to develop online communities, Palloff and Pratt's book begins with a section concentrating on the philosophy and mechanics of developing communities online, then explores hands-on methods for nurturing those communities. It also includes explicit guidance on how to inspire collaboration in online settings.

The Synchronous Trainer's Survival Guide, by Jennifer Hofmann (San Francisco: Pfeiffer, 2004)—Written primarily for those involved in training-teaching-learning, this wonderful resource serves a far larger audience by offering sections on managing, facilitating, and communicating in online spaces; managing the technology you are using; and working with live audiences online.

TED Talks: The Official TED Guide to Public Speaking, by Chris Anderson (New York: Mariner Books, 2016)—The head of TED (Technology, Entertainment, and Design) offers reflections on the foundations of public speaking (including "four talk styles to avoid" and guidance on identifying the story at the heart of the presentation you are preparing), the tools of public speaking, a review of elements of the preparation process, and plenty of tips on what to do while you are interacting with those to whom you are speaking.

Speak for a Living (Second Edition), by Anne Bruce and Sardék Love (Alexandria: ATD Press, 2018)—Although the authors have written this book for those who want to build a profitable career in public speaking, they provide plenty of useful, encouraging guidance to anyone committed to effectively serving and engaging with audiences.

If teleconferencing is the overall generic playing field for this endeavor of virtually erasing distances between participants in meetings and other conversations, telepresence is the subcategory through which effective use of online collaborative audio-video tools virtually erases geographic distance. I have, for more than a decade, been exploring this possibility with colleagues throughout the United States and other parts of the world—and the good news is that it is far easier than it initially appears to be. With Internet access, a standard laptop computer that includes a webcam and microphone, an inexpensive portable small set of speakers connected to the laptop, and a moderately priced projector (mine cost less than $500, and there are certainly less expensive options available), I'm able to quickly and easily connect onsite and online participants in ways that allow us to forget about the technology that is enabling our conversations and focus on the conversations—and positive outcomes. With any luck, you don't even have to invest in the speakers and projector; many meeting spaces already have a speaker system and projector in place, so what you need to do well before your session begins is check that your laptop is compatible with what is in the meeting space. Do at least one practice session to be sure that your microphone picks up the voices of onsite participants who may want to interact with offsite participants through question-and-answer periods (and be ready to repeat questions that the microphone doesn't adequately relay). Also check that your speaker system carries offsite speakers' voices comfortably throughout the entire onsite meeting space, and experiment with the placement of your laptop/webcam to provide the clearest, most contrast-free video feed possible. (Watch, particularly, for strong external sources of light—windows allowing sunlight to stream into a poorly lit room, for example—that need to be remedied by simply pulling down shades and/or increasing lighting within the room to the maximum extent possible so there is an even flow of light throughout the room. The nightmare scenario is to have an onsite speaker who appears as little more than a silhouette because she or he is backlit by strong sunlight through an open window while facing a webcam positioned toward the incoming flow of light.)

There certainly are very expensive, high-end ways to produce telepresence—high-quality audio and projection systems that are designed to be used in spaces eliminating any background visual reminders that participants are not, in fact, in the same conference room or other meeting space.[10] The ever-increasing sophistication of options available and surveyed throughout this chapter, however, is a good sign that high-end applications are not essential in creating telepresence at a variety of levels now. (Among the options for good up-to-date information about telepresence developments are videoconferencing tool comparisons such as those posted by FinancesOnline[11] and articles posted on the Telepresence Options website.[12]

TELEPRESENCE: REDEFINING FACE-TO-FACE

Because fostering social change involves intense, consistent, well-directed effort to create strong communities working together to achieve a common goal, it relies on an ability to bring people together face-to-face as engagingly and effectively as possible. It is through these repeated encounters—over short as well as long periods of time—that you become comfortable working with your current and prospective partners. An often-overlooked aspect of this productive face-to-face work is that the overlap between social media tools and videoconferenc-

ing/teleconferencing tools is changing the way you experience conversations "face-to-face."

"I think out of all online tools, telepresence ones can go the furthest
in replicating face-to-face connections," Jonathan Nalder observes.
"Typing and texting and images are great, especially when the easy tech
behind sharing them means we can share so much more than previously, but without the more personal interactions that, basically, video chat
gives, it would be missing a vital element."[13]

More than a decade of exploration has convinced me that it is possible—and increasingly common—to have engaging face-to-face interactions in a variety of ways: through the traditional physical gatherings
that first come to mind when you hear the term "face-to-face"; through
one-on-one interactions using desktop computers, laptops, and mobile
devices; and through the kind of blended onsite-online interactions that
are continuing to blur the difference between commonly held concepts
of where teleconferencing ends and telepresence begins. Audiences
with which I work generally forget, within the first five minutes we are
together, that someone coming into our meeting space via Skype, Google Hangouts, Zoom, or other tools is not physically present. The ability
for us to see, hear, and interact with offsite colleagues via these tools—
and for those offsite colleagues to do the same—erases those geographic distances as long as the technology is working as it is meant to work. I
have even, while sitting in front of my tablet in my home office in San
Francisco and interacting with colleagues in a meeting room on the
other side of the country, found myself reflexively reaching out to try to
catch a pen that someone in that cross-country room inadvertently hit
and sent careening virtually toward me via my screen.

My first experience with blurring the lines between teleconferencing
(using social media videoconferencing tools to interact with others) and
telepresence (using videoconferencing tools to create the sense that all
participants are side-by-side regardless of their actual physical location)
came in 2007—a time when few of my colleagues were even considering this as a possibility. Collaborating with colleagues to design and
deliver a session within a daylong Future of Libraries conference organized by a consortium of trainers in the San Francisco Bay, I asked what
appeared to be a simple question: what would it take to use Skype for
library reference services? Finding one librarian who was doing exactly
that in an academic library in Ohio, I reached out via Skype to ask her if

she would use Skype to join us in the conference site—the 235-seat Koret Auditorium in San Francisco's main library—to demonstrate Skype's teleconferencing capabilities by using it for long-distance interactions between the presenter and the audience.[14]

Several elements combined to make that initial experiment with Skype successful and ultimately left participants feeling as if the presenter (Char Booth, who was then at Ohio University Libraries), the session facilitator (who served as the critically important bridge between Booth and the onsite audience from the stage of the auditorium), and those 235 session participants were all in the same room:

Experimentation—Booth, the facilitator, members of the conference organizing committee, and members of the San Francisco Public Library IT division set out with a clear vision of how the session should run, but without any assurance that the tools available were up to the task of producing the envisioned results.

Practice—Everyone involved in planning and producing the session set aside considerable periods of time to plan and practice so problems could be identified and resolved long before the live session began. The efforts ultimately required two two-hour sessions in the auditorium: the first was to test everything that was going to be used in the auditorium (i.e., laptop, speaker system, projection system, Skype itself, and even the lighting on the stage and in the seating area) and in Booth's office, and to do an initial rehearsal that was as close as possible to what would be produced on the day of the event. The second session was to successfully test solutions to the problems that were identified during the first session.

Backup plans and a commitment to succeed—Because no one was assured of success in this experiment, everyone had backup plans in place (a plan for running the session if the video feed did not work as expected; a way to show Booth's PowerPoint slide deck if she wasn't able to display it, via Skype, from her office; and a secondary way to provide an audio feed if the Skype audio feed was not working as expected).

—◦⁄◦⁄◦—

Ten Telepresence Tips

- Look directly into your camera, not at your screen; looking at your screen prevents you from appearing to be making eye contact with your audience.
- Use a good headset (or microphone and speakers) so you can hear and be heard clearly.
- Adjust the lighting in your room so your face is evenly lit. (You can use a small, portable household lamp set up directly behind and slightly off to one side of your computer if you need to compensate for harsh lighting contrasts in the room you are using.)
- Be hypersensitive to sounds you might otherwise ignore and avoid ambient noise as much as possible; typing on your keyboard, for example, can produce a sound reminiscent of a herd of elephants running through your room if your microphone is part of or too close to your computer.
- Use a simple background, e.g., a wall painted a single, soothing color or an uncluttered office that doesn't offer distractions to those seeing you in your video feed.
- Solicit comments from others, particularly if one person is dominating the conversation or if you find yourself doing the bulk of the talking.
- Test your social media tool(s) and equipment in conditions as close as possible to the conditions in which you will engage your audience. (If you're going to be conducting the session using Wi-Fi in your own home office, for example, conduct your practice session—or sessions—in that office, using that same Wi-Fi system and the same computer or mobile device you will use during your meeting.)
- Consider purchasing a high-quality gamer router to boost the strength and reliability of your video feed if you are using Wi-Fi, particularly in your home—and be sure to position that router in a place that is as close to your computer as possible to maximize its effectiveness.
- Have a backup plan—a second laptop, mobile phone, or tablet—ready to use when, not if, your equipment fails.
- Relax and conduct yourself as if you were physically in the same place your audience is. (When telepresence works properly, you be-

gin to forget about the technology and actually do feel as if you are sharing a space with those with whom you are interacting.)

—=Ꮗ—

The event ultimately was successful not only in helping participants understand how they could use Skype to expand the way they did reference work with those they served, but also in demonstrating how easy it was to forget that Booth was not physically onsite—because, in a very important and meaningful way, she was! The event also got me thinking about the concept of what it currently means to "meet" someone for the first time. A phone call would have put us in touch; the initial and subsequent Skype sessions made me feel as if Booth and I had met and worked as effectively as if we had physically been in the same space. When we actually were together physically at a conference months later, there was no moment of blurting out the commonly expressed phrase "Nice to finally meet you face-to-face"—because, for the two of us, that meeting had taken place via Skype, just as similar first-time meetings have continued, for more than a decade, via Skype, Google Hangouts, Zoom, Shindig, Blackboard Collaborate (for academic and other learning settings), and other social media and business videoconferencing tools I have been able to use.

I have organized and been part of numerous variations on this approach since that first session in 2007, and each one adds to the ease with which I use those tools in service of the goals I am helping others reach. Having a co-facilitator for many of these sessions has made telepresence work even more effectively for those involved. In one session, for example, I worked with chapter members of what was then the American Society for Training and Development (now ATD, the Association for Talent Development). The "presentation" team included a colleague who came into the room via Skype (Sarah Houghton, the same colleague who facilitated the Future of Libraries session in San Francisco); an onsite colleague who managed a Twitter stream—which we projected onto a screen in the onsite room we were using—to demonstrate how Twitter could be an additional way to combine onsite and offsite participants in a blended conversation; and me, as the onsite facilitator making sure all involved in that session were learning how to create a sense of telepresence through tools that were readily available to all participants. (The central piece of technology was a laptop with a good built-in microphone and webcam. We plugged the laptop into the existing sound system and projection system in that room so onsite participants could hear the offsite presenter clearly through the speakers that were embedded in the ceiling of the room, and see her through the life-sized image projected on a wall in the front of the room where she would have been standing if she had been physically present.)

"It's like a live YouTube video," Samantha Adams Becker suggests. "There are several tiers of conversations that take place. There's the main event—the discussion between presenters; there's the backchannel discussions in which audience members respond to the topics by talking amongst each other; and then there's the interaction between audience and presenters, where audience members can ask questions and instantly get them answered. From that perspective, the content of the presentation itself can be influenced by the audience and morph as it goes. It becomes a true participatory experience."[15]

<hr>

Pro Tips: Videoconferencing and Telepresence

"Pick the appropriate tool for the job at hand. . . . Sometimes, a Google Hangouts thing works great. Other times, you just need a phone and a shared document."—David Lee King, author of *Face2Face: Using Facebook, Twitter, and Other Social Media Tools to Create Great Customer Connections*

"If you want to successfully do a voice and video hangout that's not phone-based, you need to make sure people on the other end have appropriate hardware, like adequate microphones, an OK video camera, and good Wi-Fi/broadband. Otherwise, one person always sounds/looks bad, or keeps dropping off the call because of technology challenges."—David Lee King

"That whole 'face-to-face is better' thing is complete bull. Your relationships and your interactions have whatever weight of meaning that you choose to give them. If you invalidate and undercut any interactions that aren't face to face, you're not going to feel their full impact. It's like self-imposed dissociation."—Elizabeth Myers, whose use of Skype and other social media tools to interact with members of the immigrant community in Markham helped create a seventy-person walk exploring the city's Islamic community

"If you want the telepresence sessions to also become a downloadable podcast for later viewing—where people will expect a higher quality than from a purely live one-off event—then . . . technical production skills are just as important. With audio, especially, people will forgive lower-resolution video if the audio is clear and understandable, but take away good audio and no one can get value from it."—Jonathan Nalder, who works globally with social media telepresence tools to foster positive change in learning

—◦◯◦—

If you or the people with whom you are working are new to videoconferencing and telepresence, you will benefit from following what plenty of evidence-based research has suggested over a long period of time:

Start with the familiar—If your community is primarily working face-to-face, have community members gather face-to-face and bring their laptops or mobile devices with them to experiment with the telepresence tool.

Take as much time as you need to be comfortable with the technology—In making the transition from onsite face-to-face interactions to blended or completely online interactions, work with your colleagues to be sure they are comfortable moving through those transitions. It doesn't take long for most users, with proper support and encouragement, to spread their wings and fly into the online world using those tools. You will know you have been successful when you and your collaborators stop talking about the technology and focus exclusively on the conversations that produce the social change you want and have agreed to pursue.

With plenty of practice and a willingness to achieve long-term success through the short-term failures that accompany all experimentation with technology, you, too, can create innovative "face-to-face" experiences that further advance the causes you serve.

NEXT STEPS

To gain a better understanding of how the use of teleconferencing tools to create telepresence can produce positive opportunities and results for you and those you serve, please try either of the following exercises involving a step you are taking to promote a small- or large-scale change in a community with which you work:

- Schedule and lead a session (e.g., a conversation or a brief meeting designed to produce a concrete result) using the teleconferencing tool of your choice; after the session, have a brief exchange, with those who joined you, about what was successful and what could have been improved.
- Go to the ChangeTheWorld-Co community on Slack; initiate or join a discussion on that site in the channel designated for chapter 8; and respond to at least two of the responses your post inspires. (If you have not already joined that community, you can do so by contacting me directly at paul@paulsignorelli.com and including a brief—one-line—description of your interest in learning more about using social media to change the world.)

9

FOLLOW THE MONEY

Changing the World through Online Fundraising

Online fundraising platforms including GoFundMe are, when used suc-
cessfully, raising billions of dollars for small- and large-scale initiatives
designed to make positive changes for individuals and communities
throughout the world. This chapter explores how activists are incorpo-
rating GoFundMe and other platforms into their change-the-world tool
kit.

When you think about exploring how online fundraising can contribute positively to your efforts, you might want to start by spending time
online reviewing the work of former GoFundMe Chief Executive Officer Rob Solomon who, *Smart Company* suggests in a headline, "wants
to change the world."[1]

Solomon, *Smart Company* writer Denham Sadler reports in that
article, "says GoFundMe, a crowdfunding platform for personal causes,
is creating real change in the world and using the power of the startup
capital of the world for good." It is a website and an organization that
centers around the efforts of individuals willing to go online to seek
financial help from others to meet personal needs (funds for school,
funds to cover medical expenses, and myriad others) as well as larger
needs, such as obtaining millions of dollars to support the March for
Our Lives project and providing funds to families affected by the Park-
land/Marjory Stoneman Douglas High School shootings; collecting $24
million for the Time's Up Legal Defense Fund (as of January 2020) "to

provide legal support to people who have experienced sexual assault and harassment in the workplace" (the most successful GoFundMe campaign in 2018)[2] ; and helping numerous others all over the world.

As is the case with so many other social media tools you have explored, it is a service and an endeavor very much grounded in the art of inspiring action through storytelling. People are moved to contribute through the heartfelt descriptions provided by those organizing and managing the various campaigns showing how donors make positive differences through their generosity and willingness to collaborate with people they didn't previously know.

"The biggest surprise is how much positivity there is in the world," Solomon said in an interview with Shubert Koong, published on the *WePay* blog. "News cycles and the social web often present a barrage of negativity. Yet I've been surprised by just how much people are compassionate, sympathetic, and empathetic—they genuinely want to help. And the power of the people collectively—which we're happy to support—can have an impact that is massively outsized even compared to some of the largest foundations and individuals in the world."[3]

It clearly does not operate in a vacuum; the most effective campaigns, regardless of the fundraising goals set, reach potential donors through the use of a variety of other social media tools (including Twitter and Facebook), other mainstream media resources (e.g., newspaper articles; news coverage on television locally, regionally, nationally, and internationally; and radio programs), and numerous creative outreach efforts from individual to individual and organization to organization. It is one of those social media tools that can be integrated easily into other social media tools to extend the reach of the messages posted and requests made. And as is the case with any good fundraising effort, it requires honest, well-planned, and well-executed campaigns that leave no doubt as to the veracity of the stories told and the positive impacts donors can have by giving at any level that is comfortable to them.

GoFundMe also provides a magnificent infrastructure for those using its services. It offers easy-to-assimilate guidance on how to set up and manage campaigns; provides plenty of ideas on how to reach the largest possible audience for any campaign posted on the site; and maintains a dynamic set of pages listing current campaigns as well as documenting campaigns that have reached successful conclusions. It reminds you, once again, that one of the best ways to understand social media is to explore it to see how others use it successfully to further their causes and reach their goals.

Solomon's fundraising platform traces its roots back to a website, "CreateAFund," started in 2008 by GoFundMe founders Brad Damphousse and Andrew Ballester. After upgrading the site, they changed the name to GoFundMe in 2010, then "sold a majority stake in Go-FundMe to Accel Partners [where Solomon had begun working as a venture partner after serving as president and COO for Groupon and holding leadership positions with SideStep, Kayak, and Yahoo!] and Technology Crossover Ventures."[4] Solomon left Accel Partners shortly after that acquisition and became CEO and Chairman during a period when donations through GoFundMe had reached $1 billion, from a total of 11.9 million different donors to one million campaigns, over a five-year period—making the site "the world's largest crowdfunding platform."[5] During his first nine months as CEO, he saw donations double (to $2 billion).[6] By the end of 2019, the organization had been the conduit for raising more than $9 billion through more than 120 million donations, according to GoFundMe's 2019 annual report.[7]

"We're going to evolve from crowdfunding to just becoming the world's largest site for giving," he predicted during a session at Startup Grind Global 2016—a goal he appears to have reached, according to a comparison of online fundraising sites updated by Crowdfunding in March 2019.[8] (GoFundMe, at that point, had passed the $5 billion mark in its fundraising efforts.)

One of the most appealing aspects of the GoFundMe approach is that it is not exclusively focused on the large-scale change-the-world causes that usually come to mind when you think about fostering social change. It very much explores and fosters connections between strangers while demonstrating the differences individuals can make for individuals in need—through the scalability of efforts.

An example cited by Solomon during his Startup Grind session involved James Robertson, a fifty-six-year-old factory worker in Detroit who could not afford to buy a car, so was walking twenty-one miles every day to go to work and return home—leaving him with just a couple of hours every night to sleep before beginning another excruciatingly long walk and workday.[9] Evan Leedy, a nineteen-year-old who became familiar with Robertson's story, was moved by Robertson's plight and his commitment to not losing the job he had struggled to obtain, so he started a GoFundMe campaign with a $25,000 goal to help Robertson buy a car and obtain payments for automobile insurance for at least a few months. Donations began pouring in almost immediately, and by the time the campaign was terminated fifty-one months later, more than 13,000 people had donated a total of $350,044 to change Robertson's world in a positive way—and brought Leedy and Robertson together at a personal level that would never have occurred if GoFundMe hadn't been, and provided, a vehicle to connect them.[10]

This obviously does not mean that every GoFundMe campaign organizer and recipient produces a story with a completely happy ending, as Rachel Monroe writes in an article for *The Atlantic*. Organizer Matt White and recipient Chauncy Black, for example, initially gained international attention when White's GoFundMe campaign raised more than $10,000 for Black in its first week of activity and eventually attracted more than $100,000 in support, but "Matt's relationship with the Blacks grew strained over time," eventually leading to reconnections between Matt White and Chauncy Black while Monroe was doing interviews for her story, she reports.[11]

Plenty of encouraging—and deeply moving—examples of GoFundMe successes are available through GoFundMe's *Medium* site,[12] with special sections for "GoFundMe Heroes,"[13] "GoFundMe Kid Heroes,"[14] and "Community"[15] stories.

There is, for example, the story of Luis Garcia, a retired firefighter/paramedic in South Florida who had administered over 3,000 doses of Narcan as part of his efforts to help individuals affected by the opioid crisis in the United States.

"After he retired, he learned that the FDA approved a nasal spray called Narcan that literally brings people back from the dead minutes after they stop breathing, with no side effects. Luis knew that this was the way to save his community. So he took the $40k that he'd been saving for a new car and went out and bought 800 doses of the nasal spray—to hand out for free," the *Medium* article reports.[16]

He also started the GoFundMe campaign that had, by January 2020, raised more than $50,000 toward his $100,000 goal to fund "a two-year mission [beginning in January 2019] to travel to the areas of America where Narcan resources are lacking."[17]

—⟡⟡⟡—

Ten Online Fundraising Tips

1. *Work with your board, organizing committee, or core group of supporters to create a simple, realistic, well-focused fundraising plan (with actions and deadlines explicitly included) that you and your colleagues can easily implement online* and *offline.* (You will find plenty of guidance by simply doing an online search using the phrase "create a fundraising plan" or by visiting your local public library onsite or online to access resources available through the library.) Integrating that fundraising plan into overall strategic and marketing plans increases your chances for success.

2. *Be among the first donors to your own campaign*, which demonstrates that you are personally invested in what you are doing.

3. *Build relationships* that help your donors see themselves as your partners in creating the change you are proposing to make. Successful fundraising often offers potential donors an opportunity to accomplish something they want to accomplish rather than making them feel as if they are nothing more than an ATM.

4. *Tell your story briefly and engagingly*—in ways that demonstrate, for current and prospective donors, how their contributions to your campaign foster positive changes in their community.

5. *Be sure you are using your other social media tools to promote your online fundraising efforts.*

6. *Keep it personal.* Simply posting your appeal and then sitting back while waiting for results rarely works. Strong, successful campaigns involve plenty of outreach and person-to-person contact online and face-to-face.

7. *Fire on all cylinders.* Don't rely solely on online fundraising to provide the financial resources you need. This means integrating your online efforts into numerous other opportunities available to you (e.g., face-to-face contact with prospective individual supporters as well as those who are leaders in your community; small- and large-scale events that draw supporters together in ways that expand your donor and project-support base; and grants from foundations and other organizations that have an affinity for the work you are doing).

8. *Build on your successes* by encouraging those who donate to your campaign to reach out to their family members, friends, and colleagues who might be equally interested in supporting your efforts. You do not have to—and cannot—do everything yourself. Fundraising is essentially community-building.

9. *Learn from others* by talking to those who have completed successful fundraising campaigns and reading their own descriptions of how they achieved success—then adapt those lessons to your own efforts. Again, you are not alone and do not need to start from scratch.

10. *Thank your donors and keep them up to date on the results they are helping produce.* Receiving a donation is part of a potentially fruitful relationship with members of your community, not the culmination of your efforts.

———

Another example, highlighting the efforts of a much younger activist, is provided by eleven-year-old Ruby Kate Chitsey, who surpassed her $250,000 goal "to help thousands of nursing home patients who are low on family and low on funds." She was moved to action one day as she was concluding a visit to one of the nursing homes where her mother works. As she left, Chitsey became engaged in a brief conversation with a resident who was sad because she could not often afford to pay the $12 it would cost to have a pet sitter bring her dog to the facility for a visit.

"I'm eleven and I have enough money saved in my piggy bank to get Pearl a few visits with her dog," Chitsey recalls thinking. She also realized that there were probably many other nursing home residents who, for lack of small amounts of cash, were foregoing experiences and small items ranging from clothing and food—Vienna Sausage turned out to be one very popular request—to access to phones for private conversations with their loved ones. Her response was to ask residents what they would want if she could bring them three things—in essence, grant them three wishes. The support she received from more than 6,000 people in a five-month period are well-documented on her GoFundMe site and provide inspiration for anyone needing a lesson in how small, incremental steps produce large, positive results through the efforts of activists like Ruby Kate Chitsey.[18]

A final example—but certainly not the last of the numerous inspirational stories available through GoFundMe—involves Equality Florida's two-part campaign to change the world for those impacted by the June 12, 2016 shooting that killed 49 people in Pulse, a gay nightclub in Orlando. Activists initially used GoFundMe to raise more than $7.5 million for the families of the shooting victims and for survivors "dealing with the physical and emotional pain of being targeted in the worst anti-LGBTQ hate crime in U.S. history."[19]

After concluding that campaign and disbursing those funds, they moved into the second of a two-phase project to change their world: they started a GoFundMe campaign to raise $375,000 to be used in "uprooting the anti-LGBTQ animosity that leads to harassment, discrimination and violence by changing the culture in schools."

"According to the Centers for Disease Control and Prevention, the two most important factors contributing to the wellbeing of an LGBTQ young person are family acceptance and a supportive school environment. Equality Florida and our partners have invested deeply in launching a Safe and Healthy Schools Project to do everything we can to prevent bigotry from taking root in our young people's hearts and minds," Nadine Smith, CEO of Equality Florida writes on the campaign site, which had attracted more than $275,000 by January 2020.[20]

An obvious lesson learned from the GoFundMe stories is that small dreams and plenty of hard work can and often do produce huge results. The remainder of this chapter provides you with an introduction to fundraising and offers guidance on how online platforms like GoFund-Me can help you obtain the funding that supports the changes you are attempting to foster.

INTRODUCTION TO FUNDRAISING

Successful fundraising has always involved offering someone an invitation to pursue an appealing opportunity as much as it involves direct requests for financial support. If you focus solely on asking potential donors for money (or in-kind donations of services and resources needed to achieve your goals), you are missing the much larger, much more rewarding opportunity to build a sustainable community capable of repeatedly producing results you might not initially imagine. If, on the other hand, your outreach concisely describes the problems you are attempting to address and engagingly focuses on the concrete positive results you are attempting to produce for individuals and groups in small as well as extended communities, your fundraising efforts produce far more than money; they create a sustainable community that repeatedly steps up to the plate when collaborative efforts are necessary.

The San Francisco Hidden Garden Steps project (see chapters 2, "The Pros and Cons of Facebook," and chapter 6, "Blogging for Social Change"), which I helped initiate in 2010 to transform a neglected, blighted 148-step set of concrete stairs in San Francisco's Inner Sunset District into a site with a ceramic-tile mosaic and adjacent gardens, shows how this works. Our four-year effort to create a safe, attractive public-meeting place that draws in visitors from all over the world involved four yearlong incremental and interwoven efforts:

Year One—Much of the work completed during this year focused on planning and organizing, which included everything from creating a formal organizing committee and obtaining a fiscal agent (the San Francisco Parks Alliance) so that there was no need to create a new nonprofit—501(c)3—organization to creating marketing and fundraising plans. It wasn't until the final month of that first year that the first donation was sought and obtained: $10,000 from two neighbors committed to seeing the project completed.

Year Two—Project volunteers engaged intensively face-to-face and online to create broad-based awareness of and enthusiasm for the project; fundraising grew slowly, incrementally, and steadily, and partnerships with local business representatives and other community leaders provided resources and added credibility to the effort.

Year Three—Donations continued to increase steadily, and the project continued to attract donors into other roles, including efforts to establish sample gardens onsite long before project artists Aileen Barr and Colette Crutcher—who served on the organizing committee from its inception even though the formal contracts for the artwork weren't completed until enough funding was in place to guarantee payment to them for their efforts—began fabricating the 148 individual pieces installed on those 148 concrete steps.

Year Four—Fundraising concluded with far more cash and in-kind services than had initially been sought, so upgrades (including extensive terracing for the hillside gardens) produced results far beyond anything initially envisioned by members of the organizing committee and other members of the global community that contributed to the success of that "neighborhood" project.[21]

One real strength of that effort to change one small piece of a very big world was that there were no silos, and project volunteers maintained a high commitment to transparency with members of their community throughout the duration of that four-year project. Members of the organizing committee met monthly (generally face-to-face, but occasionally including participation via Skype), for ninety minutes, so everyone had a clear picture of what had been accomplished and what needed to be done next. Community members who were not formally on the organizing committee attended some of those meetings when their interests and availability attracted them to specific tasks that required attention beyond what organizing committee members could do. One of the garden volunteers, for example, attended meetings while designing and completing two online fundraising efforts (one through Kickstarter and one through Indiegogo; please see the Spotlight section on Indiegogo and Kickstarter in this chapter for more information on how those platforms might fit into your online fundraising efforts) to seek money for small portions of the overall project.

What this approach produced, beyond the necessary funding, was a sense of community that had not previously existed in the neighborhood. People who had not known one another at the beginning of the project continued to meet and talk on the Hidden Garden Steps (and elsewhere) after the installation of the mosaic was completed; share information face-to-face and online (through a Facebook group) about other neighborhood projects; and work together in smaller groups when they are attracted to other community-based projects contributing to positive change through collaborative efforts.

Successful fundraising, therefore, can and should be seen as being about far more than the money raised—although you never want to lose sight of that primary goal regardless of where it leads you. It is part of an interwoven process of creating collaborative approaches for you and others who want to contribute whatever time and energy you can spare to help create the world of your dreams—and the relationships that make those efforts possible.

———❧———

Indiegogo and Kickstarter

While GoFundMe currently stands out as a primary online fundraising platform for community-based activists, it is far from the only one available. Indiegogo and Kickstarter are among those that are heavily used and well-respected, although they tend to focus more on the work of entrepreneurs or those seeking funding for arts projects—which means that if your project has an arts component, as the San Francisco Hidden Garden Steps project did, these can be alternatives well worth exploring.

Each platform has its own approach to service fees and the timing of the disbursement of funds raised. Kickstarter, for example, does not disburse funds unless the campaign's goal is reached within the timeframe allotted to the campaign; if the goal is not reached, the donors' credit cards are not charged. Indiegogo, on the other hand, does not require that the entire fundraising goal be reached before recipients can begin accessing the funds.

To be sure you have up-to-date information on these aspects of the platforms' offerings, please visit their sites.

More information is available in Stacey Nguyen's "The 7 Best Crowdfunding Sites of 2020"[22] and John-Michael Bond's "Which Crowdfunding Site Is Right for You?"[23]

———❧———

INCORPORATING GOFUNDME INTO YOUR WORK

The more you learn about the online fundraising successes of the Marjory Stoneman Douglas High School students in the days and weeks immediately following the shooting at their school in Parkland, Florida, the more you appreciate all the hard work and organizational development effort that goes into a fundraising campaign of any size. The students, in many ways, were well-prepared to draw upon numerous experiences and resources under the worst of circumstances. Some of them were media savvy because they were involved in school journalism efforts and were incorporating social media tools into those efforts. Some understood the importance and power of good storytelling because they were involved in amateur theater productions at school and in their community. Some had a keen interest in the world around them and, through their curriculum, had honed the communication skills necessary to discuss social issues in ways that touched those listening to them. And although they consistently worked to keep their peers at the center of all that they did rather than letting their efforts be heavily guided or influenced by adults, they understood that the expertise the adults around them could provide would be critically important to their success—particularly when the initial small-scale donations quickly were augmented by $500,000 donations from adults moved by their cause. When they needed to establish a nonprofit foundation to manage those funds, they were well-supported by those around them.

It is probably obvious to you at this point that there are numerous levels of sophistication with which you can approach online fundraising. If you are engaged in a short-term effort with a relatively low fundraising goal, you can probably easily manage most of your efforts through GoFundMe or other online platforms without needing to establish a formal organization to provide the complex infrastructure needed for more large-scale efforts. If you are tackling a larger project (e.g., the four-year-long Hidden Garden Steps project described earlier in this chapter) but are not interested in creating a separate nonprofit organization designed to last beyond the time it takes you to reach your current goal, you can avoid the complications by finding a fiscal agent—an existing nonprofit organization that can serve as an umbrella for your group (as the San Francisco Parks Alliance did for the Hidden Garden Steps project). If you have identified a large-scale challenge that does require formation of a formal nonprofit organization, you will benefit from the experience of others in your community who have already walked the path you are about to walk.

—◁∘∘∘▷—

Five Online Fundraising Success Stories Worth Watching

- "Boynton Beach Man [Luis Garcia] Is GoFundMe Hero for Narcan Handout," https://youtu.be/grpM1TADy0U[24]

- "Honor the Victims of Pulse Tragedy with Action," https://www.youtube.com/watch?v=UA37B-UyTVI[25]
- "Parkland HS Student Cameron Kasky Speaks at March for Our Lives Rally," https://www.youtube.com/watch?v=s7L1jFog8zE[26]
- "Three Wishes [Ruby's Residents]," https://www.youtube.com/watch?v=ccsWGC35A60[27]
- "Tile the Hidden Garden Steps & Honor LGBTs," https://www.kickstarter.com/projects/2143716381/tile-the-hidden-garden-steps-and-honor-glbts[28]

———∽∽∽———

Regardless of the level of sophistication you are pursuing, you will find plenty of great books on how nonprofits are established and sustained, and you can learn quite a bit from some of the more detailed offerings about fundraising overall (not just fundraising online), such as Kim Klein's *Fundraising for Social Change* (7th ed.)[29] and *Hank Rosso's Achieving Excellence in Fundraising* (2nd ed.),[30] edited by Eugene R. Tempel. Dave Cullen's wonderful book *Parkland: Birth of a Movement*[31] is also a tremendous resource in terms of taking you inside the March for Our Lives movement to show how the students' efforts in organizing, raising funds, organizing events, and evolving to respond to the changing set of opportunities available to them led to the successes they have achieved.

There is, however, no need to feel overwhelmed by all this information. You can start by turning to online resources available through GoFundMe. Staff members within the organization make it fairly easy for you to quickly learn what you need to know about effectively using that platform as part of your overall fundraising efforts. Using the site's extensive Help Center, you can navigate your way through a series of resource pages, beginning with one that describes, step by step, what you need to do initially while "creating a GoFundMe from start to finish."[32] That particular document ends with the reminder that "sharing is the key part to getting donations on GoFundMe. If you aren't sharing your fundraiser with your friends and family, then it's likely not going to get donations. Using your personal network can help get you closer to your goal."

Moving to the "Fundraising Tips from 7 Top GoFundMe Organizers" posted on GoFundMe's *Medium* site[33] carries you farther into the GoFundMe community by showing you what some of GoFundMe's "top organizers" recommend:

1. Push past the nervousness.
2. Be detailed in your campaign.
3. Have a clear goal in mind.
4. Share on social media.
5. Post frequent updates.
6. Add photos and videos.
7. It's OK to ask for help.

Before you actually begin creating your GoFundMe site, you should gather the materials and resources you will need to build it. Having done that, you will find the process moves smoothly and effectively—because you have engaged in the rudimentary steps of establishing the first draft of a fundraising plan designed to produce positive results.

GoFundMe has also instituted a GoFundMe Guarantee designed to help assure donors and beneficiaries that funds will be used as promised through its campaigns: "GoFundMe's mission is to empower people to help people. We want to make sure that our community feels secure during every step of the giving experience so more people can get help. The GoFundMe Guarantee is here to protect donors (those who give money to a campaign) and beneficiaries (the intended recipient of the campaign funds other than the campaign organizer) in the very rare instances of misuse," company representatives explain on their website.[34]

It received quite a bit of attention in early 2019 when the company reimbursed donors who had contributed more than $400,000 to a campaign ostensibly designed to support a homeless man who "purportedly gave his last $20 to help a stranded motorist on a Pennsylvania freeway ramp in November 2017."[35] The homeless man and the two people who solicited the funds through GoFundMe were formally charged with second-degree theft by deception and conspiracy to commit theft by deception, and two of those involved pleaded guilty, in March 2019, to one count of conspiracy to commit money laundering.[36]

The guarantee, in early 2019, covered campaigns in the United States, Canada, the United Kingdom, Germany, Spain, France, Italy, Australia, and the Netherlands. You can check the organization's website for updates on coverage (and limitations of that coverage) and for details on how to use the guarantee if you discover irregularities during your campaign.

———◦◦◦———

Pro Tips: Online Fundraising

"If you have a very clear story to tell that is concise and inspiring, it's worth pursuing; however, you can't just put some words and images on a page and expect dollars to come rolling in."—Samantha Adams Becker, consultant, who has used Indiegogo in online fundraising

"We have to lead people through a whole ladder-of-engagement process in order to get people ready to take action. For example, it would be hard to get someone to make a donation to EveryLibrary if they didn't first know who we were, our history of success, our vision for a better future—and [have] some trust and lines of communication."— Patrick Sweeney, whose work with EveryLibrary has raised funds for numerous libraries

———◦◦◦———

NEXT STEPS

To gain a better understanding of how the use of GoFundMe and other online fundraising tools can produce positive opportunities and results for you and those you serve, please try either of the following exercises involving a step you are taking to promote a small- or large-scale change in a community with which you work:

- Create a GoFundMe (or other online fundraising) campaign designed to raise funds for one specific part of your overall fundraising campaign (e.g., for a special event that draws members of your community together to further your overall project campaign and goals).

- Go to the ChangeTheWorld-Co community on Slack; initiate or join a discussion on that site in the channel designated for chapter 9; and respond to at least two of the responses your post inspires. (If you have not already joined that community, you can do so by contacting me directly at paul@paulsignorelli.com and including a brief—one-line—description of your interest in learning more about using social media to change the world.)

10

FACING INCIVILITY

Trolls, Online Harassment, and Fake News

Incorporating social media tools into your efforts to change the world will, naturally, spur opposition at a variety of levels—the worst of which includes trolling and fake news posts designed to damage your positive reputation and hinder your ability to continue the work you are doing. This chapter explores how trolls and others engaged in online harassment can affect you, and includes steps you can take to avoid being overwhelmed by those extreme challenges.

When you think about the stories you have heard or read regarding online harassment through social media, you can easily make the mistake of thinking it won't affect you. You might even unconsciously—as I have occasionally and unexpectedly found myself doing—mistakenly assume that those who are on the receiving end of trolling and other forms of online harassment are only the highly visible world-changers taking controversial stands (as if that somehow fully explains why they are being harassed).

If you follow social media at all, you know that many of the people mentioned in this book—those affiliated with Black Lives Matter, March for Our Lives, and Me Too, for example—have been subjected to trolling and other forms of harassment that are vicious, tenacious, threatening, and, at times, emotionally overwhelming. It interferes with their ability to continue or complete their work. It leaves them emotionally drained and feeling isolated. And it takes a toll on those around them, including family, friends, co-workers, and employers.

What you might have missed is the fact that plenty of others who are attempting to foster positive change in their communities through what they see as routine, uncontroversial actions have been equally traumatized by those who oppose them or simply take pleasure in provoking strong emotional responses among those they perceive to be weak, appropriate targets to torment. A study released by ADL (the Anti-Defamation League) in October 2019 suggests that more than a third of all Americans have "experienced severe online harassment"—which means that you don't have to look very far to find someone who has had this experience (if it hasn't already happened to you).[1] And if you are at all confused by what a troll is and what behavior helps you identify a troll, you'll find Todd Clarke's list of "5 signs you're dealing with a troll" helpful in making that identification: "(1) They'll try to make you angry. (2) They act entitled. (3) They exaggerate. (4) They make it personal. (5) They often can't spell."[2]

One of the most surprising set of targets I have encountered included several librarians who were simply doing what librarians do: fostering positive change within their communities by responding to the needs of library users and colleagues through the creation and posting of resources to help them find information they need. (I first heard their stories while attending the panel discussion "Bullying, Trolling, and Doxxing, Oh My! Protecting Our Advocacy and Public Discourse around Diversity and Social Justice" at the 2018 American Library Association annual conference in New Orleans.) Two of the librarians had received an American Library Association 2017 Diversity Research Grant for a project to be called "Minority Student Experiences with Racial Microaggressions in the Academic Library." The study was designed to use "surveys and focus groups to garner further insight into the specific experiences surrounding racial microaggressions directed at racial and ethnic minority students in the context of accessing library spaces and services on campus,"[3] but was abandoned "[b]ecause of the level of harassment" directed at one of the librarians.[4] Another of the librarians had tried to explain to colleagues, through a relatively brief (nine-paragraph) blog posting, what she called "race fatigue"—the "physical, mental, and emotional condition that people of color experience after spending a considerable amount of time dealing with the

micro- and macro-aggressions that inevitably occur when in the presence of white people"[5]—in an effort to make her colleagues aware of
the situation and in the hope that something positive would come from
recognition and discussion of that situation.[6] A fourth librarian—working in a college library—had published an online document designed to
"provide general information about anti-oppression, diversity, and inclusion as well as information and resources for the social justice issues
key to current dialogues" within the college community.[7]

When the reaction of those who wanted to torment each of the
librarians began to hit, several of the recipients of trolling and other
forms of online harassment were stunned and transformed by what they
experienced, they said. They were "doxxed"—their contact and other
personal information (e.g., email addresses, home addresses, and home
phone numbers) were widely disseminated online as part of a campaign
to not only discredit them but also to interfere with the work they were
doing. And, in some ways, it worked. At least one of them asked her
employers to remove her contact information from her university's
website—a process that took far longer than expected because no one
seemed to be prepared for the trauma that the librarian was experiencing as a result of a weeks-long barrage of threats and hate mail, nor was
anyone quite sure of how to respond expeditiously to the request. A few
of the librarians sought help from a variety of sources, including members of police departments, but found that support was lacking because
no actual crimes had been committed by those threatening (rather than
actually committing) acts of violence against the librarians and their
families.

A fifth librarian (who was originally scheduled to be part of a panel
discussion I attended, but ended up telling her story online after she
was unable to attend the conference) offered a bit of positive news: her
employer was behind her all the way from the time the harassment
began.

"Thankfully, and much to my honest surprise, my employer had my
back," she wrote in a piece posted on *Medium*.[8]

She also noted that the level of harassment she experienced was
much less than what her colleagues at the ALA conference described:

> I did not get death threats; and my experience was in no way com-
> pared to what Professor Taylor received. My name appeared on sev-

eral conservative forums, some now defunct. I remember reading some that encouraged readers to send me Tweets, emails, and phone calls and supplied all the necessary information to do so. There was one that was especially violent.[9]

The specific actions another of the librarians faced have been well described by Phil Morehart in *American Libraries* magazine:

> In the weeks that followed . . . , [her] email address and phone number were disseminated by hate groups and their online followers, leading to harassing phone calls and emails. When she asked for her contact information to be removed from the university's website, [she] said she received pushback from both administration and campus police.[10]

Reasons for delayed responses in these bouts with harassment varied, but a common theme among the librarians and others subjected to online harassments is the belief that "[o]ur institutions and our profession are not prepared or equipped to protect us."[11] This does not mean that those organizations remain impervious to change. A representative from one of the librarians' universities later noted:

> The personal and professional challenges experienced by [the librarian] and other faculty and staff led our university to develop new policies and resources to support victims of trolling attacks. . . . We are committed to protecting the academic freedom of our faculty members. We want to ensure that they are able to pursue their scholarship on important subjects, even if some might disagree with their work or conclusions.[12]

What all of this suggests is that in preparing for that awful moment when—not if—you are on the receiving end of trolling or other forms of online harassment, you need not feel as if you are alone. There are steps you can take to lessen the trauma and frustration harassment is designed to provoke, and you can draw upon your community of support to help you through the experience in ways that allow you to continue engaging in positive actions to help change your world.

Among the recommendations from many recipients of trolling and other forms of harassment are "don't feed the troll"—meaning that you should not engage, because engagement encourages more harassment, as you'll see in the next sections. Seeking support from friends and colleagues who provide much-needed relief when the harassment is at its worst is another recommendation repeatedly made by those who have been in that situation. And taking positive steps to not cave in to the pressure and withdraw from what you are doing helps you recover some of what you lose when you face the trauma of online harassment.

The rest of this chapter takes you into a study of what motivates trolls. It provides examples of how others in a variety of contexts have responded and survived short- and long-term online harassment, and it gives you resources that you can use now to better prepare yourself for the actions you might take when faced with online harassment. The goal remains to keep you active in your efforts to use social media (and other) tools to change your world.

———◦/◦/◦———

ADL's *The Trolls Are Organized*

"Online hate stokes fear, silences voices and causes harm to people's personal and professional lives," the authors of the ADL publication *The Trolls Are Organized and Everyone's a Target : The Effects of Online Hate and Harassment* write.[13] The report, posted online in October 2019, is just one of the numerous first-rate resources available on the topic—and it brings the issue to life through the case studies that provide the foundation of the report.

The fifteen interviewees whose comments form the core of the report show the wide range of people subjected to online harassment: those interviewees include people from a variety of ethnic backgrounds (white, Black, Latinx, and Asian) and occupations (researchers/academics, players and designers from the gaming industry, media professionals, business owners, and a worker from a social justice nonprofit). Motivations for harassment included harming a target's opportunities for employment.

"Overall, we found that it required very little to be targeted online," the authors note. Key findings included in the report are the following:

- Online hate incidents are frequently connected to the target's identity.
- Harassers use platform design to their advantage.

- Online hate can cause significant emotional and economic damage.
- Harassers also attack and impact others in the target's community (including relatives, friends, and employers).
- Social media platforms are not adequately designed to remove or efficiently review hateful content.

Interviewees who had been targeted by trolls "described their experiences as stressful and demoralizing, often isolating and traumatizing, and sometimes fear-inducing," the authors report. Some recipients of intense levels of harassment even responded by installing security systems in their homes and hiring security guards. One of the more disruptive—and dangerous—methods used by trolls in extreme cases is "swatting," defined as "the act of falsely reporting a serious crime [in progress] with the aim of drawing a massive police response to the home of an unsuspecting target."

The Trolls Are Organized concludes with three formal recommendations drawn from the interviews included in the report: (1) "increase users' control over their online space"; (2) "improve the harassment reporting process"; and (3) "build anti-hate principles into the hiring and design process." The authors also suggest that "Federal and state governments should strengthen laws that protect targets of online hate and harassment," noting that gaps in the laws allow trolling and other forms of harassment to continue—to the detriment of the trolls' targets and to those who lose the positive results the recipients of trolling might otherwise have produced if they had not withdrawn from their work under the pressure of the harassment they experienced.

ONLINE HARASSMENT THROUGH TROLLING AND FAKE NEWS

You might not initially be inclined to put the terms "trolls" and "fake news" into the same sentence, but you won't need much time to realize that both have plenty in common. They can tremendously dampen or kill your enthusiasm, pull your attention away from what you want and need to be doing, and hinder your ability to foster positive change in your world—if you let them. The impact trolls can have on you—as you saw in the introduction to this chapter—can be both overwhelming and mystifying. If there is any solace to be found in this situation, it comes from the realization that you are far from alone. Zeynep Tufekci, in her first-rate study of social media in large-scale networked protest movements, notes that the anonymity behind which many trolls hide, combined with a "laissez-faire environment" maintained by those providing social media platforms, "fosters other threats."[14] After writing about a "prominent Turkish literary figure" who received daily rape threats and death threats from hundreds of people, Tufekci notes, "I have heard or read similar sentiments from almost every prominent activist. A Black Lives Matter activist with hundreds of thousands of followers tweeted that he had blocked more than ten thousand people, and that there were many people who 'sat in his mentions' all day, meaning that they kept 'pinging' him on Twitter by using his handle, showing up on his notification tab (if they weren't blocked). . . . It is not humanly possible to stare at such threats and to casually brush them off every time."[15]

The fundamental question you want to ask when being trolled is "Why would someone do that?" The same question comes up when you find yourself serving as the subject of fake news postings—which, for those attempting to foster positive change that others may not see as positive, can include fabricated stories designed to undercut your credibility with current and prospective members of your community.

What makes online harassers create and disseminate, via social media platforms, (completely false) stories that the survivors of the Parkland shootings are actors, not students attempting to foster positive action as a result of the devastating experiences they had? What causes them to inaccurately apply the word "terrorists" to those who are attempting, through Black Lives Matter, to call attention to and chip away at actions that threaten individuals and communities? What makes them feel justified in doxxing librarians and others who are making good-faith efforts to meet the needs of the communities they serve? What makes them believe, for even a moment, that it is in any way acceptable to engage in online verbal attacks on teens who are gaining attention and respect for efforts to inspire positive change in response to challenges ranging from violence in schools to climate change?

Trying to understand why trolls engage in the incredibly asocial and destructive behavior they exhibit could fill an entire book—which is exactly what Whitney Phillips, an assistant professor of literary studies and writing at Mercer University, proved in *This Is Why We Can't Have Nice Things: Mapping the Relationship between Online Trolling and Mainstream Culture*.[16] Phillips took on the challenge of immersing herself in troll communities to better understand what motivates them and to place their behavior within the larger context of mainstream culture. She also, as her subtitle implies, links this behavior back to behavior that significant numbers of people seem to accept as "normal"—in spite of how far astream is takes you from what constitutes behavior grounded in civility. The resulting work is often difficult to read because it so effectively captures the cruelty and complete lack of empathy behind the thought processes of those who, as she notes, "take perverse joy in ruining complete strangers' days. They will do and say absolutely anything to accomplish this objective, and in the service of these nefarious ends deliberately target the most vulnerable—or as the trolls would say, exploitable—targets."[17]

You can spend hours reading and absorbing the thoughtful—and disturbing—analysis Phillips provides. You can explore, with her, the work of psychologists who, in 2014, tested "their hypothesis that trolling was a manifestation of the so-called Dark Tetrad of noxious personality traits, namely Machiavellianism, narcissism, psychopathy, and sadistic personality."[18] You can read Pierluigi Paganini's "psychology of trolls & cyberstalkers" comments and learn that "[r]esearchers from Winnipeg found clear evidence that trolling is associated specifically with sadism and to a lesser degree with Machiavellianism. The researchers also found that trolls who admit to being sadistic report that they tend to troll because they find it to be pleasurable."[19] You can even, however reluctantly, follow Phillips down the path of seeing "at bottom, the troll problem isn't a troll problem at all. It's a culture problem, immediately complicating any solution that mistakes the symptom for the disease"[20] —a suggestion you can understand, even if you aren't inclined to accept it, within the context of a period of time in which a person elected to the highest office in the United States is routinely referred to as the "troll in chief"[21] for his incessant attacks via Twitter upon those with whom he disagrees, including a sixteen-year-old climate-change activist (Greta Thunberg), who was named *Time's* Person of the Year in 2019 for her attempts to foster positive change globally.[22] There is, Phillips maintains, "a through line in the trolls' targeting practices: the concept of exploitability. Trolls believe that nothing should be taken seriously, and therefore regard public displays of sentimentality, political conviction, and/or ideological rigidity as a call to trolling arms"[23]—which is used to justify online behavior that "celebrates the anguish of the laughed-at victim."[24]

What you are left with after all that effort, however, is not much different than what you probably had when you started that exploration: a sense that trolling and online harassment goes beyond anything even remotely approaching civility and traditionally acceptable behavior—an extreme version of antisocial interaction in a disturbing world of antisocial media. What you are left with, if you are strong enough to continue the work you are so passionately pursuing while facing that level of antagonism, is a commitment to focus on your goals and not succumb to the incivility that is so prevalent online—and face-to-face.

Six Tips for Dealing with Trolls

Do not respond directly to trolls. "Trolls operate on the principle that negative attention is better than none," Nate Silver notes in a FiveThirtyEight column from 2015. "In fact, the troll may feed off the negative attention, claiming it makes him a victim and proves that everyone is out to get him."[25] They want attention; you decrease their pleasure by not providing any.

Make your colleagues and social-media followers aware of what you are facing. The March for Our Lives activists have been particularly effective in "calling out these trolls, and they're calling out these conspiracy theorists, and they're meeting this stuff head on," *Buzzfeed News* media editor Craig Silverman notes in an interview with Brent Bambury.[26]

Report trolling and other forms of harassment to representatives of the social media platforms where the harassment is occurring. While this can be time-consuming and can produce results far less effective and satisfying than you want and expect, it is one step you can take to avoid feeling you are completely powerless and to avoid succumbing to depression.

Use settings within your social media platforms to block those who are trolling you. If you put barriers between yourself and those who are harassing you, you have taken another step in the process of reducing the distractions and anguish full-fledged trolling can produce.

Have a trusted friend or colleague skim your Twitter feed and delete harassing material before you begin to use that account each day. This is another way to reduce the chance for trolls to distract you from the positive results you are attempting to promote.

Keep copies of posts that are particularly egregious and repetitive if you intend and are able to take legal actions against those whose behavior can be identified as a criminal offense. While trolling and doxxing are not generally seen as prosecutable offenses, there are times when they do lead to acts that can be handled by law enforcement officials and through the judicial system. (Pierluigi Paganini's "Trolling, Doxing & Cyberstalking: Cybercrime & the Law" offers a concise, helpful overview of "the range of threats and the challenges they present for law enforcement."[27])

———※※※———

The situation is not much better, nor any more encouraging, in the increasingly common world of fake news. When you examine the world of fake news as a subset of your overall media environment, you'll find a world where those opposed to changes proposed by activists try to undercut the activists' work by posting disturbingly inaccurate stories designed to harm the positive reputations those activists have—and the work they are doing to change the world.

March for Our Lives activists David and Lauren Hogg, for example, note that fake news posts in the form of conspiracy theories directed toward parents whose children were murdered in the Sandy Hook Elementary School shooting in December 2012[28] were quickly replicated shortly after the shootings at Marjory Stoneman Douglas High School in February 2018.

"The conspiracy theorists had already started in on us. . . . Kids were literally still looking for their parents outside the school when the trolls on 4chan started saying Parkland was a 'false flag' and we were all actors. There isn't a single person my age who doesn't know who Alex Jones [a troll who was eventually banned from Facebook, Twitter, and YouTube for his egregious online behavior[29]] is and what he did to the Sandy Hook families, so that was no surprise."[30]

Climate activist Greta Thunberg has found herself on the receiving end of similar efforts to discredit her, including false claims that she is "mentally ill, a supporter of the Islamic State terrorist group or financier George Soros' granddaughter"; that her father "live[s] in Germany with a boyfriend and her mother is . . . a Satanic lesbian who teaches teenagers about abortion"; that she "is a fictional character being played by an Australian child actress named Estella Renee"; and that she is a "puppet in the hands of a PR company."[31]

"The attacks against her have mostly avoided facts about climate science and instead gone after Thunberg, her family and her motives. They include doctored photos, threats of violence and conspiracy theories and attacks that range from the kooky to the absurd to the scary," Elizabeth Weise writes in the *USA Today* report that documented the false claims made against her.[32]

Patrisse Khan-Cullors, a co-founder of Black Lives Matter, is another activist subjected to false claims designed to discredit her and the movement with which she works. She recalls being falsely labeled a terrorist by those opposing her efforts on behalf of her community; she has also been subjected to numerous threats of violence.

"As soon as #BlackLivesMatter began trending on social media in 2013, the death threats against me began. Since then, not a week has gone by where I don't receive some threat against my life online. . . . I know firsthand what it meant to be called a terrorist after I spoke out against police violence. It meant that I became a target," she recalls in an opinion piece for CNN.[33]

Among the challenges facing those who are targets of fake news postings are several enormous issues: how social media fits into the overall media landscape, expectations held regarding the role of media serving the public interest, how expectations for accuracy in traditional media are lost within social media as an element of the overall media/information landscape, and how difficult it can be for many people to even identify whether sources they encounter are reliable. These topics are explored masterfully by Philip Napoli in *Social Media and the Public Interest: Media Regulation in the Disinformation Age.*[34] From discussions as to whether social media companies are media companies or tech companies to how First Amendment protections apply to social media platforms, Napoli consistently focuses on how adherence to concepts of "the public interest" might carry over to social media platforms.

He suggests that "the public interest principle has been systematically diminished and marginalized within the context of social media governance."[35]

"Over the past decade, it has become clear that the Internet and social media have not made everyone a journalist any more than they have made everyone a lawyer, or everyone a neurosurgeon," Napoli writes in the concluding paragraph of his book. "The pendulum needs to swing the other way, with the reestablishment and recognition of clear lines of distinction separating legitimate news and journalists from the vast oceans of content that might contain some superficial characteristics of journalism."[36]

If you want to change the world, you need to also change the way your environment looks. This means you also, at a level that is comfortable for you, have to be part of a large movement to strive for and display civility to change the tragically poor levels of discourse that occur online and face-to-face on a daily basis. Patrisse Kahn-Cullors, David and Lauren Hogg, DeRay Mckesson, Hannah Alper, Greta Thunberg, and so many others you have encountered in this book remain active on Twitter and in other efforts designed to foster discourse to promote positive change. Kahn-Cullors co-wrote *When They Call You a Terrorist* in a way that lacks bitterness and, instead, concludes with a direct challenge to "children and young people" to realize "[y]ou have the power to shape-shift not only yourselves but the whole of the world. You, each one, are endowed with gifts you don't even yet know, and you, each one, are what love and the possibility of a world in which our lives truly matter looks like."[37] DeRay Mckesson reminds you that "[h]ope is the belief that our tomorrows can be better than our todays."[38] Hannah Alper fills *Momentus* with positively inspirational stories and concludes by suggesting "[t]here's no action too small. No one sets out to change the world. . . . It's not just my actions that add up to big change. It's yours. It's ours. We're in this together."[39] And Greta Thunberg acknowledges the impact harassment and trolling can have, but manages to explain it away in a fashion that helps her stay focused on what she is attempting to accomplish: "It's of course annoying that people spend their time doing things like this when they could be doing something useful instead. . . . But there will always be people who find something to complain about."[40]

With their examples as a guiding light, you can be part of an effort to make it clear that the behavior of a "troll in chief" should not set the tenor for, or in any way be used as justification for, all public discourse—online as well as face-to-face. And it means that your efforts have to start at home: avoid the temptation to respond in kind to those who troll you or engage in any other form of harassment directed at you; avoid the temptation to troll or harass others, regardless of how much you think they deserve that awful treatment in response to what they are doing or have done; and remember that if you are part of an effort to make positive changes in your world through social media, your own ability to remain positive even under the most challenging of situations can be one of your greatest strengths.

—◦❧◦—

Pro Tips: Online Harassment

"Know the difference between a thoughtless comment and cyberbullying/trolling. Because social media can feel largely 'live' and synchronous, often people type before thinking. It happens to the best of us. However, cyberbullying is a serious offense with serious ramifications, and it is a cause that is dear to my heart. I stand with people and organizations who are working to shut it down and educate people on the repercussions."[41]—Samantha Adams Becker, consultant, whose social media posts have fostered growth within online communities

"We can all try to take the high road when trollish behavior is involved. The high road is hard as hell—believe me—but is begrudgingly worth it in the long run."[42]—Maurice Coleman, who as host of the *T Is for Training* podcast has dealt with trolling during his recordings

"You probably have to say something about developing a thick skin, ignoring the words, etc. It's really hard to do! I can type the appropriate response, but the words stay awhile longer, in reality."[43]—David Lee King, author of *Face2Face: Using Facebook, Twitter, and Other Social Media Tools to Create Great Customer Connections*

"I'm all about turning something challenging into an opportunity. If something bad happens to you on social media, channel it into spreading good. Maybe it becomes part of your story and part of your mission."[44]—Samantha Adams Becker

NEXT STEPS

To gain a better understanding of how to move past the challenges of online harassment, please try either of the following exercises:

- Read the ADL publication *The Trolls Are Organized and Everyone's a Target*; choose one of the three recommendations on pages 24–26; briefly (250 words or less) describe how you will apply that recommendation within your own change-the-world endeavors; and share that description with members of your community to foster discussion and positive action.
- Go to the ChangeTheWorld-Co community on Slack; initiate or join a discussion on that site in the channel designated for chapter 10; and respond to at least two of the responses your post inspires. (If you have not already joined that community, you can do so by contacting me directly at paul@paulsignorelli.com and including a brief—one-line—description of your interest in learning more about using social media to change the world.)

11

ORGANIZING TO CHANGE THE WORLD

Successfully incorporating social media tools into your work involves much more than simply posting and then waiting for results. The same strong organizational skills required for any change-the-world effort apply here. This chapter explores how activists combine strong organizational skills with collaborations that flow seamlessly between onsite and online settings to produce positive results.

It should be clear to you, at this point, that there is much more to social media than simply posting and waiting for results. The best efforts—including many of those highlighted in this book—often combine first-rate communication skills online as well as onsite with tremendous organizational skills and organizational development. #BlackLivesMatter without the Black Lives Matter organization[1] would be a far less influential movement than it is. #ClimateStrike, with the Global Climate Strike organization,[2] offers a combined online meeting place and onsite local chapters throughout the world to continue its work to foster positive responses to the global climate crisis, which is also promoted online through #FridaysForFuture[3] and its online map of onsite events.[4] #DACA takes on a real-world physical presence, through the support of more than 1,400 organizations and individuals,[5] in its efforts to support undocumented immigrants who want to continue living in the United States. #MarchForOurLives benefitted and continues to benefit from the deft combination of a broad-based organization[6] designed to reduce gun violence and online posts from organizers and supporters. #MeToo would be much the poorer if it didn't have the organizational prowess of the local and national organizations providing services to survivors of sexual violence[7] and of Tarana Burke's Just Be Inc., created to support young women of color "with the range of issues teen and pre-teen girls are faced with daily"[8] more than a decade before her #MeToo hashtag went viral. #WomensMarch, with its broad-based network of trainings, programs, and events, drives the movement to "harness the political power of diverse women and their communities to create transformative social change."[9]

The connections between the stories of March for Our Lives and Fridays for Future provide particularly noteworthy examples of how quick, consistent attention to the complementary nature of online and onsite (blended) interactions, and onsite-online organizational skills, led to successes for both groups. The process of creating a strong, sustainable March for Our Lives movement and organization—described earlier in this book in chapters 5 ("Picturing Change") and 9 ("Follow the Money") and well documented in Dave Cullen's book *Parkland: Birth of a Movement*[10] and Lauren and David Hogg's book *#NeverAgain: A New Generation Draws the Line*[11]—rose out of the activists' almost immediate recognition that building a strong organization would be essential to success. As noted in chapter 9, they drew upon experienced, knowledgeable supporters to help them after quickly recognizing that they needed to establish a nonprofit foundation to manage the large donations made in support of their efforts. Inspired by March for Our Lives and an earlier protest, in which students stayed away from school to stage a "climate strike" timed to coincide with the opening day of the 2015 United Nations Climate Change conference in Paris,[12] Greta Thunberg began her school strike—an initially solitary effort calling attention to climate change—by standing alone (with a handmade sign in hand) in front of the parliament building in her own country in August 2018. Recognizing that she would need a well-run organization to support her efforts, she established Fridays for Future that month. She continued to combine her onsite efforts with online posts (through Twitter,[13] Facebook,[14] and Instagram[15]) to call attention to her climate strike—an effort that steadily attracted a growing, yet relatively small group of supporters. The moment of transformation in terms of the amount of attention she was drawing to her cause came when that combined onsite-online effort led her to the opportunity to address members of the United Nations later that year, when she was fifteen years old. Attention through mainstream media outlets and a tremendous number of responses via Twitter (going from a few thousand responses on Twitter before the UN speech to more than 483,000 mentions by August 2019) allowed her to make "an unquestionable impact," and "nowhere is that more apparent than on social media," Paul Herrera notes in an article for Maven Road.[16]

But it's not just about attention and reach; it's also about the concrete results produced through those well-organized, blended efforts. When you look at what March for Our Lives has helped produce, you see changes in legislation at the state and national levels,[17] growing support nationally for positive actions to reduce violence involving the use of guns,[18] and efforts to register and engage new voters in the electoral process.[19] When you look at Climate Strike, you see that the first sixteen months of activities put Thunberg in conversation with world leaders willing to support positive responses to the effects of climate change and "inspired 4 million people to join the global climate strike on September 20, 2019, in what was the largest climate demonstration in human history."[20] Those marches, executed with a scope and efficiency reminiscent of the Women's March and March for Our Lives efforts, spurred action by students "in 2,233 cities and towns in 128 countries, with demonstrations held from Australia to India, the UK and the US."[21]

ORGANIZING FOR SUCCESS THROUGH COMMUNITY AND COLLABORATION

At the heart of all this is community—onsite, online, and at the level of the blended efforts so frequently apparent as you engage in your own world-changing efforts and as you follow the work of those you admire for their world-changing actions. It is at least partially fostered through the recognition, described in the "Telepresence: Redefining Face-to-Face" section of chapter 8 ("Videoconferencing and Telepresence"), that you can use some of your social media and other tech tools to create engaging, dynamic, productive interactions that strengthen the ability of your community to continue doing your work—just as members of the #etmooc (Educational Technology & Media massive open online course)[22] community continued to do in January 2020 through the group's *seventh* annual online reunion that keeps that global teaching-training-learning community intact and looking for ways to produce positive results for the learners its members serve. Members of the ShapingEDU community do the same through monthly online gatherings[23] that continue conversations connected to those held during its annual "Unconference for Dreamers, Doers, and Drivers Shaping the Future of Learning in the Digital Age,"[24] just as members of the Elders Action Network do through online community conversations and workshops.[25] These are not the splashy, viral, well-recognized efforts that gain plenty of media attention; they are the day-to-day efforts of people who often don't see themselves as activists but, rather, as members of communities striving to produce the small-scale changes that lead to cumulative successes at a larger level.

❦❦❦

Peter Block and John McKnight on Building Abundant Communities

Attending a community-building session led by writer-consultant Peter Block in 2008, I was struck by how effectively Block worked with the 250 of us in that large room to demonstrate how easy it was to begin building connections between people who gather with a common purpose or commitment in place. He initiated the session by encouraging us, within two two-minute periods of time and with explicitly clear instruction, to reset the seating arrangements in that massive hall (which could have easily held three times the number of attendees who were actually present) in a way that we thought would better facilitate our learning. At the end of that brief exercise, he had transformed us from a group of loosely connected colleagues into a temporary community of learning that was prepared for and excited by the prospect of working together to better learn how to organize the communities we served.

Block, with his Abundant Community partner John McKnight, remains one of the finest community facilitators I have encountered—one who effectively speaks to and writes about the art of organizing highly functioning communities and identifying community resources you might otherwise overlook. His *Community: The Structure of Belonging*[26] offers a tremendous roadmap to building community through extended sections on "The Fabric of Community" and "The Alchemy of Belonging," offering plenty of tips that can be used onsite as well as online. Returning to the topic in *The Abundant Community: Awakening the Power of Families and Neighborhoods*,[27] he (with McKnight) provides abundant inspiration for identifying and incorporating possibly overlooked partners into your change-the-world efforts—a process which continues through the Abundant Community website[28] and interactive webinars they offer.

If you're interested in learning more about—and joining those efforts to build—abundant communities, you'll find Block and McKnight on their website at https://www.abundantcommunity.com, which includes links to their blog and archived recordings of the webcasts.

Tips designed to create, nurture, and sustain these blended communities dedicated to changing the world are remarkably parallel to the online-fundraising tips offered in chapter 9. These tips include establishing organizational plans—with strong mission, vision, and value statements—that help keep community efforts focused and measurable in terms of achievements versus goals that remain unreached. They include a commitment to building relationships that allow your colleagues and supporters to see themselves as your partners in creating the change you are proposing to make. They are centered around a commitment and ability to tell your story briefly and engagingly through all means available to you onsite and online—in ways that are personal and invitational rather than coldly factual and distant. They are built upon an understanding that change—small-scale as well as large-scale—is a step-by-step process that requires building upon the successes you achieve and that are not derailed by the inevitable setbacks, opposition, and even harassment you and your colleagues will face. They include a commitment to learning from others—those who support you as well as those who oppose what you are attempting to accomplish—with a well-maintained commitment to empathy so you can understand why others might not be as enamored of what you are attempting to do as you are. And they require a strong commitment to frequently thanking those who support you and doing everything you can to keep those supporters informed, involved, and energized—actions that take you far beyond any mistaken belief that social media is a magic bullet that, once fired, resolves everything you and members of your community are attempting to resolve.

You know you have a strong community worth sustaining when you have established beliefs and goals that are shared throughout that community, e.g., a commitment to civil discourse; a commitment to continue working toward your goals until you reach them; a commitment to addressing, to the best of your ability, the concerns expressed by those who are—at least for now—opposed to what you are proposing; and a well-developed, collaboratively created process for resolving conflicts among members of your community. You know you have a strong community worth sustaining when you are more focused on producing positive results than on engaging in trolling and putting the majority of your efforts on discrediting those with whom you do not agree. You know you have a strong community when disagreements are resolved amicably and in ways that strengthen the community's ability to foster the positive changes it is committed to making rather than resulting in incessant squabbles that drain the community of its greatest resources: collaboration, determination, and focus.

The result, in the best of situations, is a seamless blending of online and onsite interactions rather than interactions that focus on online rather than onsite activities—or vice versa. To engage effectively is to engage through every means possible—"to fire on all cylinders," as one of my cherished fundraising mentors, Robert Zimmerman, repeatedly reminded me over a long period of time.

——◆◆◆——

On Building Effective Communities of Practice

It may feel a bit strange at first to learn about community-building by reviewing how nearly two dozen members of an online community in which I am active collaborated as co-authors to produce and publish a guide to building effective communities. Taking a behind-the-scenes look at the creation and publication of *Building Effective Communities of Practice*,[29] however, draws together themes discussed in this chapter. It also introduces you to practices that can help you better develop the support you need to reach your change-the-world goals.

Building Effective Communities, above all, is a change-the-world attempt to help others learn from educators-as-activists who have successfully developed and sustained communities of practice designed to nurture positive change among their members and other learners. These communities of practice—generally defined as groups of people with a shared interest or affinity (e.g., a profession) and drawn together through engagement or shared activity to achieve specific, well-defined results—have much in common with groups developed to foster positive change locally, regionally, nationally, or globally.

Drafted in its early stages as a collaboration between colleagues in ShapingEDU and Penn State's CoAction Learning Lab in mid-2019, the draft really began to come to life when it was introduced to ShapingEDU community members during a ninety-minute, highly interactive ShapingEDU webinar.[30] Participants in that webinar, after making informal contributions to the document (which existed in an online collaboration tool), were invited to continue adding to it and shaping it.

The posted publication has plenty to offer in terms of helping to define communities of practice. It provides best practices in areas including diversity and inclusion, engagement and collaboration, experience and leadership, shared values and purpose, and structure and processes. The publication also offers a variety of examples, including case studies, and concludes with references and additional resources that can help you more successfully reach your own goals through the support and engagement of a highly functioning community. The following are keys to its successful completion and publication:

- a couple of ShapingEDU members who were in charge of overseeing creation, editing, and publication of the finished product;
- clearly defined goals and deadlines to be followed by those of us who contributed to the document;[31]
- an online platform that was easy to use, familiar to co-authors, and readily accessible; and
- plenty of opportunities for interactions—synchronous as well as asynchronous—among contributors.

The resulting guide is well-researched, practical, and engaging because it contains plenty of anecdotes as well as clear-cut guidance on how to develop and sustain communities of practice. Most importantly, it is readily accessible at the moment of need to members of communities of practice as well as to members of communities attempting to foster positive change. You can use it and even contribute to it with suggestions including additional best practices and examples through the document home page at https://shapingedu.asu.edu/communities-of-practice.

—◦◦◦—

You will, as you delve ever deeper into what leads to success and what leads to setbacks in efforts to change the world through the use of social media, find increasingly sophisticated assertions of what is possible—and find that not all social media users are in agreement as to the efficacy of the platforms you have been exploring throughout this book. Jen Schradie, for example (in *The Revolution That Wasn't: How Digital Activism Favors Conservatives*), provides a well-researched case study that suggests social media outlets are far less effective at creating a level playing field than you might have been led to expect.[32] One of the many notable points she makes throughout the book is how conservatives, in the situation she studies, use better organizational skills and greater access to resources than their liberal counterparts do—to the detriment of the liberals *in that situation*. Three other professors—Sarah Jackson, Moya Bailey, and Brooke Foucault Welles—on the other hand, "argue that by effectively coupling the speed of communication on the internet with *careful organization* [italics mine], activist efforts organized online can potentially build inclusive, connected movements with a speed and magnitude possibly not accessible—or even imaginable—to earlier generations of organizers"[33] —as you have seen throughout *Change the World*.

COMMITMENT TO WORK, COMMITMENT TO SUCCESS

In this chapter and throughout this book, you have encountered numerous examples of how social media platforms can be part of your successful change-the-world efforts. The tools continue to evolve, but the underlying commitments are consistent: you identify the tool or tools that most effectively work for you and are most likely to be used by those with whom you are—or want to be—working; you bring, to your efforts, the best of the organizational skills you have and the best onsite and online resources available; you tell the best stories you can tell; you maintain the most positive approach possible to all that you do; and you find success by listening as much as you speak so that you facilitate productive conversations and actions within communities capable of fostering the results that draw you and your partners together.

As Schradie reminds you near the beginning of *The Revolution That Wasn't*, "digital activism takes work, and work takes organization. The social movement groups with the capacity to do digital work had more complex organizational infrastructure. It takes this infrastructure to develop, and especially maintain, digital use and participation."[34] It also, as you have seen throughout *Change the World*, takes passionate, determined, creative, skilled, empathetic individuals willing to adopt a step-by-step approach to work toward creating the world of their dreams.

Best of luck in your efforts to be among that change-the-world cohort at the local, regional, national, and international level. With social media tools as part of your tool kit, you will never be alone.

———〰〰〰———

Pro Tips: Building Community through Social Media

"Be bold. Be brave. Be vulnerable. Share your story. It's the simple truths that are often most striking. In order to really connect with people, you need to open up. Don't just talk; listen."—Samantha Adams Becker, consultant, whose social media posts have fostered growth within online communities

"Like any good organizer, you use all of the tools available to you to get your message out. You shouldn't care about the method, just care about the message and make it clear, concise, and as honest as you can—and be willing to repeat it over and over and over and over and over and over and over and over again. Remember that people listen in small bursts."—Maurice Coleman, whose biweekly *T Is for Training* podcast has been inspiring positive change among trainer-teacher-learner-doers since 2008

"To use social [media] effectively, you need intention. What is your intention? Why are you there on that platform? Where should you be?"—Jill Hurst-Wahl, whose work has facilitated productive engage-

ment among members of nonprofit organizations she has joined and
served

"Be consistent, and share from the heart. *If* you are authentic in your
meaning and motive, it will come out positive, even if it's not something
everyone is interested in. Then consistently *keep* sharing, and, eventually, it might just happen."—David Lee King, author of *Face2Face: Using
Facebook, Twitter, and Other Social Media Tools to Create Great Customer Connections*

"[Don't] try to be someone you're not. It sounds really basic but it's
actually very hard, because in some ways the social media popularity
contest is about performing an identity on the Internet. But finding
ways to genuinely be who you are while connecting with people is
critical."—Cayden Mak, Executive Director of 18 Million Rising

"Do unto others! Basically, don't treat it as a one-way broadcast platform. Reach out. Support others."—Jonathan Nalder, who through FutureWe uses social media tools as a conduit to a global community of
educators exploring and promoting positive change in training-teaching-learning

"Don't see, or use, social media as an end-all tool. It's really great for a
lot of things, but it has to be a part of a more holistic approach to social
change."—Patrick Sweeney, political director for EveryLibrary, which
builds voter support for libraries

NEXT STEPS

To gain a better understanding of how to organize and best incorporate
the social media tools available to you into your day-to-day work, please
try any of the following three exercises:

- Work with colleagues to define the strengths and weaknesses of
  one change-the-world effort you are currently pursuing. Then determine how the use of at least one social media tool might help
  better take advantage of your strengths or overcome a weakness.
  Create a short (one page or less) description outlining steps you

will take and the deadline(s) by which you will complete the action(s) you are proposing, and post that brief action plan in the ChangeTheWorld-Co community on Slack. (If you have not already joined that community, you can do so by contacting me directly at paul@paulsignorelli.com and including a brief—one-line—description of your interest in learning more about using social media to change the world.)

- Initiate or join a discussion on the ChangeTheWorld-Co Slack community in the channel designated for chapter 11; respond to at least two of the responses your post inspires.
- Develop—or if you already have them in place, use existing—mission, vision, and value statements designed to help you reach your goals, and identify one action you will take within the next two weeks to use a social media tool in support of those mission, vision, and value statements.

GLOSSARY

Note: Wikipedia (www.wikipedia.org) is a recommended resource for further information about many of the terms and tools included in this glossary. URLs at the end of entries lead to the tool under consideration.

algorithm: a precise set of instructions used to guide a computer as it completes a set of computations, e.g., the set of instructions created by programmers at **Facebook** to determine which of your friends' posts you see when you use your Facebook account and which of your friends' posts are excluded when you are using your Facebook account.

backchannel: an informal, online forum for conversation, generally organized around a **hashtag** via **Twitter** or other **social media** tools, between people attending events (e.g., conferences or political rallies) onsite or online; among the participants are those reacting to events based on the online comments and coverage they see.

Bitly: a service that shortens the number of letters, numbers, and symbols needed in a **URL** to reach a specific website; this tool is useful when creating web addresses that are to be used in **tweets** or other short forms of online communication. (*See also* TinyURL.) https:// bitly.com/

blended communication: exchanges, using online tools, between a group of people who are physically together in one location and those who are elsewhere, e.g., an individual in one physical setting using an online tool to communicate with a group of individuals who are some-where else and, simultaneously, collaborating together in their shared physical space. (*See also* telepresence *and* videoconferencing.)

blog: an online platform (a "weblog") for writing and posting content you want to share with others online; blog platforms have evolved to allow writers to integrate imagery and links to videos and other online content into their online posts. (*See also* Blogger, blogging, Medium, microblogging, Tumblr, *and* WordPress.)

Blogger: an online platform for creating and maintaining a **blog**. (*See also* blogging, Medium, microblogging, Tumblr, *and* WordPress.) https://www.blogger.com/

blogging: originally from the term "weblog" to indicate the personal nature of this approach to writing and posting content online (in "per-sonal logs" or diaries), this form of writing has expanded richly and extensively to include content ranging from short in-the-moment pieces of writing to more thoughtful, well-researched writing that in the best of situations rivals professionally published content—because it is writ-ten and posted online by professional writers. (*See also* blog, Blogger, Medium, microblogging, Tumblr, *and* WordPress.)

bot: a software robot (i.e., software) designed to repeatedly and rapidly engage in large-scale online transactions; chatbots, for example, are designed to provide online assistance in a variety of settings, while spambots are designed to generate unsolicited online messages via email, **Twitter**, and other platforms. (*See also* spam.)

Chatter: an online collaboration, communication, and project-manage-ment tool that allows members of a group to engage in text-based con-versations that are organized, maintained, and archived by topic. (*See also* Jive, Slack, Trello, *and* Yammer.) https://www.salesforce.com/prod ucts/chatter/overview/

community of practice: a group of people drawn together by a com-mon interest and a commitment to achieve goals and objectives deter-mined by its members.

Creative Commons licensing: an avenue for exerting control over content you have created and want to share online. https://creative commons.org/licenses/

cyberbullying: engaging in bullying or other forms of harassment online. (*See also* doxing/doxxing *and* trolling.)

digital literacy: the ability to select and use appropriate online tools to successfully meet an information or other need.

doxing/doxxing: publishing, online, a person's contact and other personal information (e.g., email address, home address, or home phone number) with the express intention of fostering online and onsite harassment of that person. (*See also* cyberbullying.)

#etmooc: the Educational Technology & Media massive open online course originally facilitated by Alec Couros and others, from Canada, in early 2013. http://etmooc.org/sample-page/

Facebook: one of the largest, most popular **social media** platforms for staying in touch with those you know through the posting of (generally short) notes, photographs, videos, and links to online content you want to share with those to whom you are connected in this communication tool. You have some—but not absolute—control over who sees your content, but that content can be seen by others if those with whom you choose to be connected in this forum share content you have posted. https://www.facebook.com/

fake news: content that intentionally includes inaccurate information, is shared online or through traditional broadcast media intentionally, and is disseminated with the intention to mislead those who are reading/viewing/listening to that content; it can also be content that intentionally includes inaccurate information for humorous/satirical purposes.

Flickr: an online platform where you can post, share, and view photographs. https://www.flickr.com/

GoFundMe: a platform that supports online fundraising efforts. (*See also* Indiegogo *and* Kickstarter.) https://www.gofundme.com/

hashtag: a user-developed tool that allows you to follow conversations by theme or a specific word (including proper names) or group of words on **Twitter** and other **social media** platforms. (For example, if you search for "#BlackLivesMatter" on Twitter, you will see the **tweets** that include that combination of the hashtag symbol (#) and the term "BlackLivesMatter"; if you search for #DeRayMckesson, you will see the tweets that include the name DeRayMckesson when it is preceded by the # symbol and used without any space between the first and last names.) Note that the search is not case-sensitive, i.e., it works regardless of whether you use capital or lowercase letters after the # symbol.

Hootsuite: an online tool that allows you to follow multiple online feeds organized through a **hashtag**. (*See also* Tweetdeck.) https://hootsuite.com/

Indiegogo: a platform that supports online fundraising efforts. (*See also* GoFundMe *and* Kickstarter.) https://www.indiegogo.com/

Instagram: a popular **social media** platform designed primarily for the sharing of photographs and videos online; small amounts of text (i.e., **microblogging**) can be included and integrated into posts on this platform, and you can embed links to videos into your posts. https://www.instagram.com/

Jive: an online collaboration, communication, and project-management tool that allows members of a group to engage in text-based conversations that are organized, maintained, and archived by topic. (*See also* Chatter, Slack, Trello, *and* Yammer.) https://www.jivesoftware.com/

Kickstarter: a platform that supports online fundraising efforts. (*See also* GoFundMe *and* Indiegogo.) https://www.kickstarter.com/

LinkedIn: a platform used primarily to foster professional (i.e., work-related) connections online, e.g., between you and your colleagues within the industry in which you work or between employers and employees in search of each other; it can be used in activism to reach out to colleagues who may be interested in the cause you are supporting. https://www.linkedin.com/

#lrnchat: an online community of trainer-teacher-learners whose primary means of communication is through weekly facilitated online conversations via **Twitter**. (*See also* tweet chat.) https://lrnchat.wordpress.com/

Medium: an online social journalism/**blogging** platform for posting your written work. (*See also* blog, Blogger, microblogging, Tumblr, *and* WordPress.) https://medium.com/

meme: a small block of words or a small combination of words and images, often designed to be humorous or satirical, posted online to spread an idea—sometimes to provoke thought and social action.

microblogging: writing and posting relatively short (ranging from an upper limit of 280 characters per post in **Twitter** to a few paragraphs in tools such as **Tumblr**) pieces in an online platform. (*See also* blog, Blogger, blogging, Medium, *and* WordPress.)

MOOC: a massive open online course; an online, sometimes highly interactive course open free of charge to anyone interested in studying the topic to be covered; these courses sometimes attract small numbers of learners (fewer than a hundred) and sometimes attract thousands of participants. (*See also* #etmooc.)

podcast: an audio recording made, posted, and accessed online, and generally part of a series featuring a consistent host or set of hosts consistently exploring a specific theme, e.g., politics, learning, current affairs, or any other topic of interest to the target audience for the recording.

Shindig: an online **videoconferencing** tool, i.e., a tool that allows participants to see and hear one another live, online for a variety of purposes ranging from informal conversations to formal meetings and organizing/training sessions. (*See also* Skype *and* Zoom.) https://www.shindig.com/

Skype: an online **videoconferencing** tool, i.e., a tool that allows participants to see and hear one another live, online for a variety of purposes ranging from informal conversations to formal meetings and organizing/training sessions. (*See also* Shindig *and* Zoom.) https://www.skype.com

Slack: an online collaboration, communication, and project-management tool that allows members of a group to engage in text-based conversations that are organized, maintained, and archived by topic. (*See also* Chatter, Jive, Trello, *and* Yammer.) https://slack.com/

Snapchat: a popular **social media** platform designed primarily for short-term sharing of photographs and other imagery online, i.e., content that generally remains online in your account for short periods of time before being automatically deleted; small amounts of text (i.e.,

microblogging) can be included and integrated into posts on this platform, and you can embed links to videos into your posts. https://www.snapchat.com/

social media: the wide-ranging array of tools and platforms available online allowing you to connect to and interact synchronously and asynchronously with other people regardless of your and their physical locations.

spam: unsolicited online communication generally created and disseminated at a large scale via email and other online communication platforms. (*See also* bot.)

tagging: embedding key words preceded by the **hashtag** symbol (#) into your **social media** posts to help others find your content; including #MarchForOurLives in a **tweet**, for example, helps people find tweets about that movement.

TalkShoe: an online tool for creating a **podcast**. (*See also* Zencastr.) https://www.talkshoe.com/

teleconferencing: communicating with others online through the use of telecommunication tools (e.g., landlines and cell phones) that allow participants to hear and interact with one another; Wikipedia also refers to "Internet teleconferencing," which includes the video capabilities inherent to **videoconferencing**. (*See also* telepresence.)

telepresence: an approach to **videoconferencing** that focuses on creating the sense that all online participants are sharing the same physical space, e.g., a meeting room, a conference room, or a classroom.

TinyURL: a service that shortens the number of letters, numbers, and symbols needed in a **URL** to reach a specific website; this tool is useful when creating web addresses that are to be used in tweets or other short forms of online communication. (*See also* Bitly.) https://tiny url.com/

Trello: an online collaboration, communication, and project-management tool that allows members of a group to engage in text-based conversations that are organized, maintained, and archived by topic. (*See also* Chatter, Jive, Slack, *and* Yammer.) https://trello.com

troll: a person who derives pleasure from provoking strong, generally negative responses through acts of harassment online.

trolling: the act of deliberately harassing others online with the intention of provoking strong, negative reactions. (*See also* cyberbullying.)

Tumblr: an online **blogging** platform that offers various formatting options based on what type of content you want to highlight, e.g., highlighting a photograph and adding a small amount of complementary text, highlighting a video, or creating a text-based blog post supplemented by photographs or a video. (*See also* blog, Blogger, Medium, microblogging, *and* WordPress.) https://www.tumblr.com/

tweet: the act of posting a note on **Twitter**; the term is also used to refer to the posts themselves.

tweet chat: a live, online exchange/conversation conducted using **Twitter** and, generally, focused on a specific theme or topic with the assistance of a formal or informal facilitator guiding the session.

TweetDeck: an online tool that allows you to follow multiple online feeds organized through a **hashtag**. https://tweetdeck.twitter.com/

Twitter: a platform for writing and posting relatively short notes and observations containing no more than 280 characters (*not* 280 words); photographs, other images, and links to online content including videos can be added to your posts in this platform. (*See also* microblogging.) https://twitter.com/

URL: Uniform Resource Locator; a web address, i.e., the specific, unique sequence of letters, numbers, and symbols used to take you to a website.

videoconferencing: communicating with others online through the use of tools (e.g., **Skype**, **Shindig**, or **Zoom**) that allow participants to see, hear, and interact with one another. (*See also* telepresence.)

Vimeo: a **social media** platform for posting and viewing videos; users can also use the platform to post comments about the videos. (*See also* YouTube.) https://vimeo.com/

webinar: an online broadcast, with audio and video elements, that can be comprised of someone providing information to others in the form of a lecture or, in its more interactive (and effective) version, a present-er providing information and engaging with others conversationally.

Wikipedia: an online, user-generated, well-managed encyclopedia that demonstrates what a global **community of practice** can accomplish collaboratively. https://www.wikipedia.org/

WordPress: an online platform for creating and maintaining a **blog**; it is flexible enough to be used solely as a blog, as a website, or a com-bined site for your blog and website. (*See also* Blogger, blogging, Me-dium, microblogging, *and* Tumblr.) https://wordpress.com/

Yammer: a collaboration, communication, and project-management tool that allows members of a group to engage in text-based conversa-tions that are organized, maintained, and archived by topic. (*See also* Chatter, Jive, Slack, *and* Trello.) https://products.office.com/en-us/yammer/yammer-overview

YouTube: an extremely popular **social media** platform for posting and viewing videos; users can also use the platform to post comments about the videos. (*See also* Vimeo.) https://www.youtube.com/

Zencastr: an online tool for creating a **podcast**. (*See also* TalkShoe.) https://zencastr.com/

Zoom: an online **videoconferencing** tool, i.e., a tool that allows partic-ipants to see and hear one another live, online for a variety of purposes ranging from informal conversations to formal meetings and organizing/training sessions. (*See also* Shindig *and* Skype.) https://zoom.us/

NOTES

PREFACE

1. Maurice Coleman. Conversation with Paul Signorelli. February 9, 2018.
2. Wikipedia. "List of Social Networking Websites." Accessed January 9, 2020. https://en.wikipedia.org/wiki/List_of_social_networking_websites.
3. Colin Horgan. "What the Facebook, Google and Twitter Algorithms Hide from You." *Maclean's*. November 8, 2017. https://www.macleans.ca/technology-3/what-the-facebook-google-and-twitter-algorithms-hide-from-you/; Brent Barnhart. "How the Facebook Algorithm Works and Ways to Outsmart It." SproutSocial. May 31, 2019. https://sproutsocial.com/insights/facebook-algorithm/.
4. ShapingEDU. "ShapingEDU: Dreamers, Doers, and Drivers Shaping the Future of Learning in the Digital Age." Accessed January 9, 2020. https://shapingedu.asu.edu/.
5. #etmooc. "About." Accessed January 9, 2020. http://etmooc.org/sample-page/.
6. George Couros. *The Innovator's Mindset: Empower Learning, Unleash Talent, and Lead a Culture of Creativity*. San Diego: Dave Burgess Consulting, 2015.
7. Paul Signorelli. "Innovator's Mindset MOOC (#IMMOOC): Down the Blended Reading Rabbit Hole Again." *Building Creative Bridges* blog. October 10, 2017. https://buildingcreativebridges.wordpress.com/2017/10/10/innovators-mindset-mooc-immooc-down-the-blended-reading-rabbit-hole-again/.
8. Ibid., "Change the World Using Social Media." *Building Creative Bridges* blog. Accessed January 9, 2020. https://buildingcreativebridges.word press.com/category/change-the-world-using-social-media/.

I. WHAT IS SOCIAL MEDIA AND
WHAT CAN IT DO FOR YOU?

1. Cayden Mak. Interview by Paul Signorelli. December 1, 2017.

2. Wikipedia. "Social Media." Accessed January 16, 2020. https://en.wikipedia.org/wiki/Social_media.

3. Association for Psychological Science. "Social Media 'Likes' Impact Teens' Brains and Behavior." May 31, 2016. https://www.psychologicalscience.org/news/releases/social-media-likes-impact-teens-brains-and-behavior.html.

4. Pekka Ihanainen and John Moravec. "Pointillist, Cyclical, and Overlapping: Multidimensional Facets of Time in Online Learning." *The International Review of Research in Open and Distributed Learning* (November 2011). http://www.irrodl.org/index.php/irrodl/article/view/1023/2022.

5. Paul Signorelli. "Learning Time and Heads That Spin." *Building Creative Bridges* blog. March 14, 2013. https://buildingcreative-bridges.wordpress.com/2013/03/14/learning-time-and-heads-that-spin/.

6. Christian Resource Ministry. "About." Accessed January 16, 2020. https://christianresourceministry.com/serve-others/.

7. Sam Earp. Interview with Paul Signorelli. January 16, 2018.

8. Paolo Gerbaudo. *Tweets and the Streets: Social Media and Contemporary Activism.* London: Pluto, 2012.

9. Zeynep Tufekci. *Twitter and Tear Gas: The Power and Fragility of Networked Protest.* New Haven and London: Yale University, 2017.

10. Samantha Adams Becker. Interview by Paul Signorelli. November 3, 2017.

11. Everett Rogers. *Diffusion of Innovations*, 5th ed. New York: Free Press, 2003.

12. Howard Rheingold. *Net Smart: How to Thrive Online*, 2014 paperback edition. Cambridge and London: MIT, 2012.

13. Snopes. Accessed December 28, 2017. https://www.snopes.com/.

14. Donald Barclay. *Fake News, Propaganda, and Plain Old Lies: How to Find Trustworthy Information in the Digital Age.* London: Rowman & Littlefield, 2018.

2. THE PROS AND CONS OF FACEBOOK

1. Melissa Eddy. "Vienna 'New Year's Baby' Greeted First with Hate, Then Hearts." *The New York Times*. January 4, 2018. https://www.nytimes.com/2018/01/04/world/europe/vienna-new-years-baby.html.

2. Samantha Adams Becker. Interview by Paul Signorelli. January 15, 2018.

3. Tim O'Reilly. *WTF: What's the Future and Why It's Up to Us*. New York: HarperCollins, 2017.

4. Cayden Mak. Interview by Paul Signorelli. January 12, 2018.

5. Wikipedia. "Facebook." Accessed January 12, 2018. https://en.wikipedia.org/wiki/Facebook.

6. Carolyn Abram. *Facebook for Dummies*, 6th ed. New Jersey: John Wiley & Sons, 2016.

7. Facebook. "Help Center." Accessed January 12, 2018. https://www.facebook.com/help/.

8. Tony Choi. Interview by Paul Signorelli. January 12, 2018.

9. Shoshana Zuboff. *The Age of Surveillance Capitalism: The Fight for a Human Future at the New Frontier of Power*. New York: Public Affairs/Hachette, 2019.

10. Ibid., p. 301.

11. Ibid., p. 340.

12. Andrew Perrin and Monica Anderson. "Share of U.S. Adults Using Social Media, Including Facebook, Is Mostly Unchanged Since 2018." Pew Research Center. April 10, 2019. https://www.pewresearch.org/fact-tank/2019/04/10/share-of-u-s-adults-using-social-media-including-facebook-is-mostly-unchanged-since-2018/.

13. Jonathan Nalder. Interview by Paul Signorelli. November 6, 2017.

14. Greg Swan. "How the Facebook Algorithm Works + 5 Best Practices [2020]." tinuiti. April 29, 2020. https://tinuiti.com/blog/paid-social/facebook-algorithm/.

15. Casey Newton. "Facebook's Startling New Ambition Is to Shrink: A Wild Reversal Comes to the News Feed." *The Verge*, January 14, 2018. https://www.theverge.com/2018/1/14/16885314/facebook-news-feed-changes-meaningful-interactions.

16. Maurice Coleman. Interview by Paul Signorelli. December 13, 2017.

17. Becker interview.

18. David Lee King. Interview by Paul Signorelli. November 20, 2017.

19. Choi interview.

20. Paul Signorelli. "Friends of the Hidden Garden Steps: About." Accessed January 12, 2018. https://hiddengardensteps.wordpress.com/about.

21. 16th Avenue Tiled Steps. http://www.16thavenuetiledsteps.com. Accessed January 12, 2018.

22. Hidden Garden Steps Facebook Page. Accessed January 12, 2018. https://www.facebook.com/Hidden-Garden-Steps-288064457924739.

23. Wikipedia. "Third Place." Accessed January 20, 2020. https://en.wikipedia.org/wiki/Third_place.

24. *The Guardian*. "What Jobs Will Still Be Around in 20 Years? Read This to Prepare Your Future." June 26, 2017. https://www.theguardian.com/us-news/2017/jun/26/jobs-future-automation-robots-skills-creative-health.

25. Nalder interview.

26. Coleman interview.

27. Mak interview.

28. Patrick Sweeney. Interview by Paul Signorelli. March 6, 2018.

29. Ibid.

30. Ray Oldenburg. *The Great Good Place: Cafés, Coffee Shops, Bookstores, Bars, Hair Salons, and Other Hangouts at the Heart of a Community*. New York: Marlowe & Company, 1989.

31. Elizabeth Myers. Interview by Paul Signorelli. December 14, 2017.

3. TWITTER—SMALL MESSAGES
WITH LARGE RESULTS

1. Beatrice Di Caro. "#MeToo, #balancetonporc, #yotambien: Women around the World Fight Back at Harassment." World Economic Forum, October 18, 2017. https://www.weforum.org/agenda/2017/10/metoo-balance tonporc-yotambien-women-around-the-world-lash-out-at-harassment/.

2. Wikipedia. "Me Too Movement." Accessed January 19, 2018. https://en.wikipedia.org/wiki/Me_Too_movement.

3. Wikipedia. "Donald Trump *Access Hollywood* Tape." Accessed January 19, 2018. https://en.wikipedia.org/wiki/Donald_Trump_Access_Hollywood_tape.

4. Jody Kantor and Megan Twohey. "Harvey Weinstein Paid Off Sexual Harassment Accusers for Decades." *The New York Times*, October 5, 2017. https://www.nytimes.com/2017/10/05/us/harvey-weinstein-harassment-allega tions.html.

5. Ronan Farrow. "From Aggressive Overtures to Sexual Assault: Harvey Weinstein's Accusers Tell Their Stories: Multiple Women Share Harrowing Accounts of Sexual Assault and Harassment by the Film Executive." *The New Yorker*, October 10, 2017. https://www.newyorker.com/news/news-desk/from-

aggressive-overtures-to-sexual-assault-harvey-weinsteins-accusers-tell-their-stories.

6. Medium. "Chris Messina." Accessed January 19, 2018. https://medium.com/@chrismessina.

7. Chris Messina. "The Hashtag Is 10!: What the Hashtag Means to Me 10 Years after Its Invention." Medium, August 23, 2017. https://medium.com/chris-messina/hashtag10-8e114c382b06.

8. Jacquelyn Jacobsma. "Are Hashtags Still #Relevant for Your Digital Ad Content in 2020?" *9Clouds* blog. Updated January 3, 2020. https://9clouds.com/blog/are-hashtags-still-relevant-for-digital-ad-content/.

9. Cara McGoogan. "Hashtag Turns 10: Seven Facts You Didn't Know about the Trending Symbol." *The Telegraph*, August 23, 2017. http://www.telegraph.co.uk/technology/2017/08/23/hashtag-turns-10-seven-facts-didnt-know-trending-symbol/.

10. Samantha Adams Becker. Interview by Paul Signorelli. January 22, 2018.

11. Wikipedia. "Twitter." Accessed January 19, 2018. https://en.wikipedia.org/wiki/Twitter.

12. Sarah Perez. "Twitter Officially Expands Its Character Count to 280 Starting Today." *TechCrunch*, November 7, 2017. https://techcrunch.com/2017/11/07/twitter-officially-expands-its-character-count-to-280-starting-today/.

13. Wikipedia, "Twitter."

14. Internet Live Stats. "Twitter Usage Statistics." Accessed January 20, 2020. http://www.internetlivestats.com/twitter-statistics/.

15. Maurice Coleman. Interview by Paul Signorelli. January 9, 2018.

16. Jonathan Nalder. Interview by Paul Signorelli. January 31, 2018.

17. David Lee King. Interview by Paul Signorelli. January 31, 2018.

18. Cayden Mak. Interview by Paul Signorelli. January 18, 2018.

19. Jill Hurst-Wahl. Interview by Paul Signorelli. January 15, 2018.

20. Elizabeth Myers. Interview by Paul Signorelli. December 5, 2017.

21. Becker interview.

22. Coleman interview.

23. Becker interview.

24. Nalder interview.

25. Cliff Atkinson. *The Backchannel: How Audiences Are Using Twitter and Social Media and Changing Presentations Forever.* Berkeley: New Riders, 2010.

26. Paul Signorelli. *Building Creative Bridges* blog. Accessed January 22, 2018. https://buildingcreativebridges.wordpress.com/?s=backchannel.

27. King interview.

28. #lrnchat. "About #lrnchat." Accessed January 22, 2018. http://lrnchat.com/.

29. Ibid., "Transcripts." Accessed January 22, 2018. http://lrnchat.com/.

30. Steve Cooper. "The Ultimate Guide to Hosting a Tweet Chat." *Forbes*, September 30, 2013. https://www.forbes.com/sites/stevecooper/2013/09/30/the-ultimate-guide-to-hosting-a-tweet-chat/#fd2898031ee2.

31. Mak interview.

32. Nalder interview.

4. LINKEDIN AND COLLABORATIVE PROJECT-MANAGEMENT TOOLS

1. Andrew M. Calkins. "LinkedIn: Key Principles and Best Practices for Online Networking & Advocacy by Nonprofit Organizations." 2013. The Julie Belle White-Newman MAOL Leadership Award, Paper 12. Accessed March 1, 2018. https://sophia.stkate.edu/maolhonors/12/.

2. Ibid., 37.

3. Ibid., 1.

4. Ibid., 65.

5. David Lee King. Interview by Paul Signorelli. January 31, 2018.

6. Jonathan Nalder. Interview by Paul Signorelli. January 31, 2018.

7. Cayden Mak. Interview by Paul Signorelli. January 18, 2018.

8. Vartika Kashyap. *Workforce*. "28 Best Slack Alternatives for Team Communication (You Cannot Live Without)." ProofHub. March 11, 2020. https://www.proofhub.com/articles/slack-alternatives.

9. Jessica Kerr. *The Composition* blog. "Effective Use of Slack." September 22, 2017. https://the-composition.com/effective-use-of-slack-2189896aba67.

10. Lydia Dishman. "Best Practices from the Most Active Slack Users." *Fast Company*. May 7, 2015. https://www.fastcompany.com/3046011/best-practices-from-the-most-active-slack-users.

11. Jory MacKay. "How to Use Slack Effectively: 25 Slack Settings and Features That Will Save Your Focus." *RescueTime* blog. July 15, 2020. https://blog.rescuetime.com/slack-focus-guide/.

12. King interview.

13. Mak interview.

14. Jeffrey Young. "New Media Consortium Unexpectedly Shuts Down, Citing 'Errors and Omissions' by CFO." *EdSurge*. December 18, 2017. https://www.edsurge.com/news/2017-12-18-new-media-consortium-unexpectedly-shuts-down-citing-errors-and-omissions-by-cfo.

15. TIB. "NMC Horizon Report > 2017 Library Edition Now Published." March 23, 2017. https://www.tib.eu/en/service/news/details/nmc-horizon-report-2017-library-edition-now-published/.

16. LinkedIn. "Help." Accessed March 3, 2018. https://www.linkedin.com/help/linkedin/answer/2753?query=connecting%20to%20twitter.

17. Paul Signorelli. *Building Creative Bridges* blog. "Shaping Education Unconference 2018," four-part blog posting. April/May 2018. https://building creativebridges.wordpress.com/?s=shapingedu.

18. FOEcast. "About." Accessed March 8, 2018. https://www.foecast.net/about/.

19. ShapingEDU. "10 Actions to Shape the Future of Education." Accessed July 18, 2018. https://www.dropbox.com/s/ckzsoota2b6cc2g/10-Actions-to-Shape-the-Future-of-Education-2018.pdf?dl=0.

20. Samantha Adams Becker. Interview by Paul Signorelli. January 22, 2018.

21. Jeff Merrell. Interview by Paul Signorelli. February 6, 2018.

22. Jeff Merrell. *Jeff Merrell* blog. "Revisiting: A Critical Pedagogy for Organizational Learning?" January 27, 2018. https://jeffdmerrell.com/2018/01/27/revisiting-a-critical-pedagogy-for-organizational-learning/.

23. Merrell interview.

24. Merrell interview.

5. PICTURING CHANGE

1. Monica Anderson and Jingjing Jiang. "Teens, Social Media & Technology 2018." Pew Research Center. May 31, 2018. http://www.pewinternet.org/2018/05/31/teens-social-media-technology-2018/?utm_source=Pew+Research+Center&utm_campaign=88a23bc4c7-EMAIL_CAMPAIGN_2018_05_31_03_46&utm_medium=email&utm_term=0_3e953b9b70-88a23bc4c7-400448441.

2. Chris Browne. "Snapchat Footage from Marjory Stoneman Douglas High School in Parkland." YouTube. Posted February 14, 2018. https://www.youtube.com/watch?v=qOw4TdqFU-I.

3. Wikipedia. "March for Our Lives." Accessed March 28, 2019. https://en.wikipedia.org/wiki/March_for_Our_Lives.

4. *USA Today*. "Oregon Lawmakers Pass Gun-Control Bill; First Since Florida Shooting." February 23, 2018. https://www.usatoday.com/story/news/nation/2018/02/23/oregon-lawmakers-pass-gun-control-bill-after-florida-shooting/366216002/.

5. James Call. "Florida Lawmakers Send Gun-Control Bill to Governor, Includes Plan to Arm Teachers." *USA Today*. March 7, 2018. https://www.usatoday.com/story/news/politics/2018/03/07/florida-house-passes-first-gun-controls-20-years-gov-scott-wont-say-if-hell-sign/405452002/.

6. Instagram. "March for Our Lives." Accessed March 29, 2018. https://www.instagram.com/marchforourlives/?hl=en.

7. Flickr. Images gathered from a search on the term "March for Our Lives." Accessed March 29, 2018. https://www.flickr.com/search/?text=march%20for%20our%20lives.

8. Bill Chappell. "Logan Paul, YouTube Star, Apologizes as Critics Slam Video Showing Dead Body." NPR. January 2, 2018. https://www.npr.org/sections/thetwo-way/2018/01/02/575057157/logan-paul-youtube-star-apologizes-as-critics-slam-video-showing-dead-body.

9. Samantha Adams Becker. Interview by Paul Signorelli. February 27, 2018.

10. Stanford Libraries. "Copyright Reminder: Fair Use." Accessed January 21, 2020. https://library.stanford.edu/using/copyright-reminder/copyright-law-overview/fair-use.

11. Creative Commons. "About the Licenses." Accessed March 28, 2019. https://creativecommons.org/licenses/.

12. Dana Liebelson and Nick Wing. "Behind Millions of Dollars Raised by Parkland Students, An Adult Board of Directors." *HuffPost*. March 19, 2018. https://www.huffingtonpost.com/entry/march-for-our-lives-action-fund_us_5ab02dbbe4b0697dfe19a488.

13. CBS News. "Parkland Shooting Survivors Say NRA Is 'Basically Threatening' Them." March 19, 2018. https://www.cbsnews.com/news/david-hogg-emma-gonzalez-parkland-florida-shooting-survivors-nra-threats/.

14. Tufayel Ahmed. "Is Snapchat Over? Kylie Jenner Possibly Caused $1.3 Billion Loss in Value, But It's Not Dead Yet, Expert Says." *Newsweek*. February 23, 2018. http://www.newsweek.com/snapchat-over-kylie-jenner-possibly-caused-13-billion-loss-value-its-not-dead-817849.

15. Kayleigh Barber. "How *Seventeen* Is Using Snapchat to Give Young Activists a Voice." *Folio*. March 5, 2018. https://www.foliomag.com/how-seventeen-is-using-snapchat-to-give-young-activists-a-voice/.

16. Laurie Keith. "What You Didn't Know about Shapchat's Power for Social Good." ConvinceAndConvert.com. Accessed May 15, 2018. http://www.convinceandconvert.com/social-media-strategy/snapchat-social-good/.

17. Fenton staff. "Five Snapchat Campaigns for Social Change." Fenton. February 18, 2016. https://fenton.com/five-snapchat-campaigns-that-inspired-social-change/.

18. Paige Alfonzo. "Snapchat in the Library: Librarians Master an App to Reach Millennials." *American Libraries*. November 1, 2016. Accessed March 25, 2018. https://americanlibrariesmagazine.org/2016/11/01/snapchat-in-the-library/.

19. Wikipedia. "Internet Meme." Accessed March 25, 2018. https://en.wikipedia.org/wiki/Internet_meme.

20. Tony Vincent. "Infopics." Learning in Hand. Accessed March 25, 2018. https://learninginhand.com/infopics.

21. Jonathan Nalder. Interview by Paul Signorelli. January 31, 2018.

22. Sarah Ben Romdane. "5 Arab Activists Using Instagram to Push for Change." *Mille* newsletter. November 27, 2019. https://www.milleworld.com/young-arab-activists-using-instagram/.

23. Devorah Rose. "Trendy Social Activists Prove Instagram Is a Platform for More Than Selfies." *Vice*. July 26, 2017. https://impact.vice.com/en_us/article/padwxn/trendy-social-activists-prove-instagram-is-a-platform-for-more-than-selfies.

24. Founder's Guide. "Instagram for Social Good: 9 Accounts with Causes That Will Inspire You." June 27, 2016. http://foundersguide.com/instagram-for-a-cause/.

25. *Dazed*. "The Instagram Accounts Changing the World." August 9, 2015. http://www.dazeddigital.com/artsandculture/article/25814/1/the-instagram-accounts-changing-the-world.

26. David Lee King. Interview by Paul Signorelli. February 21, 2018.

27. Poor People's Campaign. Accessed March 25, 2018. https://www.poorpeoplescampaign.org/demands/.

28. Jill Hurst-Wahl. Interview by Paul Signorelli. January 15, 2018.

6. BLOGGING FOR SOCIAL CHANGE

1. Hannah Alper. *Call Me Hannah* blog. Accessed July 15, 2018. http://callmehannah.ca.s209419.gridserver.com/.

2. Hannah Alper. *Momentus: Small Acts, Big Change*. Toronto: Nelson Education, 2017.

3. Hannah Alper. "Be More Eco-Friendly for $10 and 10 Minutes." *Call Me Hannah* blog. July 19, 2012. http://callmehannah.ca/be-more-eco-friendly-for-10-and-10-minutes/.

4. WE Movement. Accessed January 27, 2020. https://www.we.org/en-US.

5. Hannah Alper. "The Top 10 Things I Found Cleaning Up Trash in the Schoolyard." *Call Me Hannah* blog. September 20, 2015. http://callmehannah.ca/the-top-10-things-i-found-cleaning-up-trash-in-the-schoolyard/.

6. Hannah Alper. "It's Not Always Sunshine and Rainbows." *Call Me Hannah* blog. September 13, 2018. http://callmehannah.ca/its-not-always-sunshine-and-rainbows/.

7. Wikipedia. "Tag (Metadata)." Accessed July 15, 2018. https://en.wikipedia.org/wiki/Tag_(metadata).

8. PCDN. "Blogging for Social Change & Impact: PCDN Resource Guide." Accessed July 15, 2018. https://pcdnetwork.org/resources/guide-to-blogging-for-peace-and-social-change/.

9. *wpbeginner* Editorial Staff. "How to Choose the Best Blogging Platform in 2020 (Compared)." January 2, 2020. https://www.wpbeginner.com/beginners-guide/how-to-choose-the-best-blogging-platform/.

10. Jill Hurst-Wahl. *Digitization 101* blog. Accessed September 11, 2018. http://hurstassociates.blogspot.com/.

11. Jill Hurst-Wahl. Interview by Paul Signorelli. September 11, 2018.

12. Samantha Adams Becker. Interview by Paul Signorelli. September 21, 2018.

13. *Friends of the Hidden Garden Steps* blog. Accessed July 15, 2018. http://hiddengardensteps.wordpress.com.

14. *T Is for Training* blog. Accessed July 15, 2018. http://tisfortraining.wordpress.com.

15. Wikipedia. "Blog." Accessed September 18, 2018. https://en.wikipedia.org/wiki/Blog.

16. Dylan Tweney. "Tim O'Reilly: Web 2.0 Is about Controlling Data." *Wired*. April 13, 2007. https://www.wired.com/2007/04/timoreilly-0413/?currentPage=2.

17. Tim O'Reilly. "Draft Blogger's Code of Conduct." *O'Reilly* blog. April 8, 2007. http://radar.oreilly.com/2007/04/draft-bloggers-code-of-conduct.html.

18. Morten Rand-Hendriksen. "Code of Ethics for Bloggers, Social Media and Content Creators." *Mor10* blog. Accessed September 18, 2018. https://mor10.com/code-of-ethics-for-bloggers-social-media-and-content-creators/.

19. "A Bloggers' Code of Ethics." CyberJournalist.net. January 1, 2003. http://cyberjournalist.net/a-bloggers-code-of-ethics.

20. Samantha Adams Becker. *Hey Kid* blog. Accessed September 11, 2018. https://oh-hey-kid.tumblr.com/.

21. Organizing for Action. Accessed September 18, 2018. http://barackobama.tumblr.com/.

22. Pekka Ihanainen and John Moravec. "Pointillist, Cyclical, and Overlapping: Multidimensional Faces of Time in Online Learning." *The International Review of Research in Open and Distributed Learning.* November 2011. http://www.irrodl.org/index.php/irrodl/article/view/1023/2022.

23. Paul Signorelli. "Learning Time and Heads That Spin." *Building Creative Bridges* blog. March 14, 2013. https://buildingcreativebridges.wordpress.com/2013/03/14/learning-time-and-heads-that-spin/.

24. Buffy Hamilton. *The Unquiet Librarian* blog. Accessed July 15, 2018. https://theunquietlibrarian.wordpress.com/.

25. Buffy Hamilton. *Living in the Layers* blog. Accessed July 15, 2018. https://livinginthelayers.com/author/buffyjhamilton/.

26. Hurst-Wahl interview, February 22, 2018.

7. BROADCASTS AND PODCASTS

1. Phillip "Brail" Watson. Facebook. Accessed October 25, 2018. https://www.facebook.com/braillionaire/.

2. Phillip "Brail" Watson. "Giving Back." TEDxTopeka. Posted on YouTube April 6, 2015. https://www.youtube.com/watch?v=hE0rXmOU1ks.

3. Paul Signorelli. "The Spread of Learning Rhizomes." *Building Creative Bridges* blog. February 14, 2012. https://buildingcreativebridges.wordpress.com/2013/02/14/the-spread-of-learning-rhizomes/.

4. Go Topeka. "Momentum 2022." Accessed September 22, 2020. https://dashboards.mysidewalk.com/momentum2022/home-b7dac3e295ef.

5. Greater Topeka Partnership. "Topeka & Shawnee County Have Momentum." Posted on YouTube May 24, 2017. https://www.youtube.com/watch?v=GSorFk1Objk.

6. Phillip "Brail" Watson. "Topeka Proud." Posted on Vimeo 2015. https://vimeo.com/141371834.

7. Greater Topeka Partnership. "#Momentum2022, Part 2." Posted on YouTube January 19, 2018. https://www.youtube.com/watch?v=9kkGtHPx1HA.

8. YouTube Creators [Creator Academy]. "Inspiring Social Change on Your Channel." Posted on YouTube February 22, 2018. https://www.youtube.com/watch?v=sDlrmcHDeYM.

9. Wikipedia. "List of Most-Subscribed YouTube Channels." Accessed November 30, 2018. https://en.wikipedia.org/wiki/List_of_most-subscribed_YouTube_channels.

10. Jeremy Vest. "15 Tips for Growing Your YouTube Channel." *Social Media Examiner.* Posted January 4, 2018. https://www.socialmediaexaminer.com/15-tips-growing-youtube-channel/.

11. Samantha Adams Becker. Interview by Paul Signorelli. March 12, 2018.

12. YouTube. "Create a New Channel." Accessed November 30, 2018. https://support.google.com/youtube/answer/1646861?hl=en.

13. Leena Normington. "Go Back to Where You Came From." Posted on YouTube September 5, 2017. https://www.youtube.com/watch?v=Lud6ttxOJro.

14. Subhi Taha. "Just Say It." Posted on YouTube September 25, 2017. https://www.youtube.com/watch?v=6TID1oxsNc0.

15. Niharika Nm. "You're Ugly." Posted on YouTube November 12, 2018. https://www.youtube.com/watch?v=TAc9h9QFlrI.

16. Becker interview.

17. Jill Hurst-Wahl. Interview by Paul Signorelli. March 15, 2018.

18. YouTube Creators Academy. "All Courses." Accessed November 30, 2018. https://creatoracademy.youtube.com/page/education.

19. YouTube Creators for Change. "50+ Films That Bring Us Together." Accessed November 20, 2018. https://www.youtube.com/channel/UCYJJ pu7FLQqu788cusj6nIg.

20. USC Price. "Highlights: The Evolution of a Social Activist (How I Found My Voice!)." Posted on YouTube November 27, 2017. https://www.youtube.com/watch?v=wI69NYOo5uM.

21. TED. "An Interview with the Founders of Black Lives Matter: Alicia Garza, Patrisse Cullors, Opal Tometi." Posted on YouTube December 20, 2016. https://www.youtube.com/watch?v=tbicAmaXYtM.

22. SoulPancake. "Kid President Asks 'What Makes an Awesome Leader?'" Posted on YouTube December 8, 2016. https://www.youtube.com/watch?v=KdL4o7wU0CQ.

23. TVO Channel Digital U. "Social Media: Online Activism." Posted January 21, 2010. https://www.youtube.com/watch?v=AN-kIJI_5wg.

24. Repairers of the Breach. "This Wall Is Sin!" Posted on YouTube October 27, 2017. https://www.youtube.com/watch?v=A7bJjMH5oPc.

25. DeRay Mckesson. *Pod Save the People.* Accessed November 13, 2018. https://crooked.com/podcast-series/pod-save-the-people/.

26. *Model MAJORITY Podcast.* "Episode 91: Profound Humanity, Profound Identity." Recorded October 14, 2018. https://www.stitcher.com/podcast/model-majority-podcast/e/56714826.

27. Jennifer Hill. *Get Yourself the Job.* "Hannah Alper." Recorded January 22, 2018. https://player.fm/series/get-yourself-the-job/hannah-alper-rqpMMpYdZcGWN2Sj.

28. Maurice Coleman. Interview by Paul Signorelli. March 29, 2018.

29. Jonathan Nalder. Interview by Paul Signorelli. March 14, 2018.

8. VIDEOCONFERENCING AND TELEPRESENCE

1. Elders Action Network. "Elder Wisdom." Accessed January 27, 2020. https://eldersaction.org/elder-wisdom/.

2. Ibid.

3. Elders Climate Action. "About Us." Accessed January 27, 2020. https://www.eldersclimateaction.org/aboutus/.

4. Sage-ing International. "About." Accessed January 24, 2019. https://www.sage-ing.org/about/.

5. Seniors Action Network. "About." Accessed January 24, 2019. https://www.leadingage.org/grassroots/seniors-action-network.

6. Elders Action Network. "EAN Community Conversations." Accessed January 27, 2020. https://www.eldersaction.net/cen_community_conversations.

7. Wikipedia. "Cloud-Based Video Conferencing." Accessed January 22, 2019. https://en.wikipedia.org/wiki/Videotelephony#Cloud-based_video_conferencing.

8. Wikipedia. "Videotelephony." Accessed January 22, 2019. https://en.wikipedia.org/wiki/Videotelephony.

9. Wikipedia. "Telepresence." Accessed January 22, 2019. https://en.wikipedia.org/wiki/Telepresence.

10. Leo Kelion. "'Hologram' Lecturers to Teach Students at Imperial College London." International Society for Presence Research. Posted November 5, 2018. https://ispr.info/2018/11/05/hologram-lecturers-to-teach-students-at-imperial-college-london/.

11. FinancesOnline. "List of Top 11 Video Conferencing Software." Updated August 18, 2020. https://communications-software.financesonline.com/c/video-conferencing-software.

12. Telepresence Options. "Home." Accessed January 25, 2019. http://www.telepresenceoptions.com/.

13. Jonathan Nalder. Interview by Paul Signorelli. March 14, 2018.

14. Paul Signorelli. "Skype as Conference Tool." *American Libraries* 32 (May 2008). http://paulsignorelli.com/PDFs/Skype%20as%20Conference%20Tool.pdf.

15. Samantha Adams Becker. Interview by Paul Signorelli. March 12, 2018.

9. FOLLOW THE MONEY

1. Denham Sadler. "How GoFundMe CEO Rob Solomon Wants to Change the World." *Smart Company.* June 24, 2016. https://www.smartcompa

ny.com.au/startupsmart/profiles/how-gofundme-ceo-rob-solomon-wants-to-change-the-world/.

2. Victoria Rodriguez. "Time's Up Tops List of Most Successful GoFund-Me Campaigns in 2018." *Mashable*. December 6, 2018. https://mashable.com/article/gofundme-top-fundraisers-campaigns/.

3. Shubert Koong. "Focus on Key Priorities—Q&A with GoFundMe's CEO Rob Solomon." *WePay* blog. July 18, 2018. https://blog.wepay.com/2018/07/18/focus-on-key-priorities-qa-with-gofundmes-ceo-rob-solomon/.

4. Wikipedia. "GoFundMe: History." Accessed March 7, 2019. https://en.wikipedia.org/wiki/GoFundMe#History.

5. Ryan Mac. "How Anti-Kickstarter GoFundMe Became the Crowdfunding King with Causes Not Projects." *Forbes*. September 24, 2015. https://www.forbes.com/sites/ryanmac/2015/09/24/gofundme-largest-crowdfunding-platform-1-billion-donations/#6d28a3f66299.

6. Startup Grind. "Rob Solomon (GoFundMe) and Ryan Sweeney (Accel Partners) at Startup Grind 2016." Posted on YouTube March 11, 2016. https://www.youtube.com/watch?v=E0aElkhmgyE.

7. GoFundMe. "GoFundMe 2019." Accessed January 23, 2020. https://www.gofundme.com/2019.

8. Crowdfunding. "Comparing the Top Online Fundraising and Crowdfunding Platforms." Updated March 25, 2019. https://www.crowdfunding.com.

9. Marisa Kabas. "Donations Pour in for Detroit Man Who Commutes 21 Miles a Day on Foot." *Today*. February 3, 2015. https://www.today.com/news/donations-pour-detroit-man-who-commutes-21-miles-day-foot-t161.

10. Evan Leedy. "Help James Robertson Get a Car." GoFundMe. Posted February 1, 2015. https://www.gofundme.com/getthisguyacar.

11. Rachel Monroe. "When GoFundMe Gets Ugly." *The Atlantic*. November 2019. https://www.theatlantic.com/magazine/archive/2019/11/gofundme-nation/598369/.

12. GoFundMe. "GoFundMe Stories" *Medium*. Accessed March 8, 2019. https://medium.com/gofundme-stories.

13. GoFundMe. "GoFundMeHeroes." *Medium*. Accessed March 8, 2019. https://medium.com/gofundme-stories/tagged/gofundme-heroes.

14. GoFundMe. "GoFundMe Kid Heroes." *Medium*. Accessed March 8, 2019. https://medium.com/gofundme-stories/tagged/gofundme-kid-heroes.

15. GoFundMe. "Community." *Medium*. Accessed March 8, 2019. https://medium.com/gofundme-stories/tagged/gofundme-community.

16. GoFundMe. "Meet Luis." *Medium*. Posted November 15, 2018. https://medium.com/gofundme-stories/meet-luis-60396d1c5379.

17. Luis Garcia. "USA Opioid Crisis Mortality Reduction with Narcan." GoFundMe. November 27, 2017. https://www.gofundme.com/f/USAOpioid-

CrisisMortalityReductionWithNARCAN?utm_source=&
utm_medium=referral&utm_content=heroes&utm_campaign=luis-garcia.

18. GoFundMe. "Three Wishes for Ruby's Residents." Posted November 21, 2018. https://www.gofundme.com/three-wishes-for-ruby039s-residents ?utm_source=medium&utm_medium=referral&utm_content=kid-heroes &utm_campaign=ruby-kate.

19. GoFundMe. "Support Victims of Pulse Shooting." Posted June 12, 2016. https://www.gofundme.com/PulseVictimsFund?utm_source=& utm_medium=referral&utm_content=comms&utm_campaign=pulse-one-year-later.

20. GoFundMe. "Honor Them with Action." Accessed May 1, 2019. https:// www.gofundme.com/forthe49.

21. Friends of the Hidden Garden Steps. "About." Accessed May 6, 2019. https://hiddengardensteps.wordpress.com/about/.

22. Stacey Nguyen. "The 7 Best Crowdfunding Sites of 2020." The Balance Small Business. November 20, 2019. https://www.thebalancesmb.com/best-crowdfunding-sites-4580494.

23. John-Michael Bond. "Which Crowdfunding Site Is Right for You?" *Daily Dot*. March 19, 2018. https://www.dailydot.com/debug/gofundme-alternatives-kickstarter-indiegogo-youcaring/.

24. WPTV News. "Boynton Beach Man Is GoFundMe Hero for Narcan Handout." Posted on YouTube December 4, 2018. https://youtu.be/ grpM1TADy0U.

25. #Forthe49. "Honor the Victims of Pulse Tragedy with Action." Posted on YouTube November 4, 2016. https://www.youtube.com/watch?v=UA37B-UyTVI.

26. WUSA9. "Parkland HS Student Cameron Kasky Speaks at March for Our Lives Rally." Posted on YouTube March 24, 2018. https:// www.youtube.com/watch?v=s7L1jFog8zE.

27. CBS Sunday Morning. "Three Wishes." Posted on YouTube March 3, 2019. https://www.youtube.com/watch?v=ccsWGC35A60.

28. Sherry Boschert. "Tile the Hidden Garden Steps & Honor LGBTs." Posted March 17, 2011. https://www.kickstarter.com/projects/2143716381/tile-the-hidden-garden-steps-and-honor-glbts.

29. Kim Klein. *Fundraising for Social Change* (7th ed.). San Francisco: Jossey-Bass, 2016.

30. Eugene Tempel, ed. *Hank Rosso's Achieving Excellence in Fundraising* (2nd ed.). San Francisco: Jossey-Bass, 2003.

31. Dave Cullen. *Parkland: Birth of a Movement*. New York: HarperCollins, 2019.

32. GoFundMe. "Creating a GoFundMe from Start to Finish." Accessed March 8, 2019. https://support.gofundme.com/hc/en-us/articles/3600019926 27-Creating-a-GoFundMe-From-Start-to-Finish.

33. GoFundMe. "Fundraising Tips from 7 Top GoFundMe Organizers." *Medium*. Posted May 10, 2017. https://medium.com/gofundme-stories/campaign-tips-from-7-top-gofundme-organizers-870de6682c44.

34. GoFundMe. "GoFundMe Guarantee FAQs." Accessed May 6, 2019. https://pages.gofundme.com/guarantee-faq/.

35. Phil Helsel. "GoFundMe Says Donations in Alleged Homeless Scam Fundraiser Returned." NBC News. December 24, 2018. https://www.nbcnews.com/news/us-news/gofundme-says-donations-alleged-homeless-scam-fundraiser-returned-n951736.

36. Janelle Griffith. "Homeless Man, N.J. Woman Accused in GoFundMe Scam Plead Guilty." NBC News. March 6, 2019. https://www.nbcnews.com/news/us-news/homeless-man-n-j-woman-accused-gofundme-scam-plead-guilty-n980166.

10. FACING INCIVILITY

1. ADL, with Danya Glabau and Jordan Kramer. *The Trolls Are Organized and Everyone's a Target: The Effects of Online Hate and Harassment*. October 2019. https://www.adl.org/media/13633/download.

2. Todd Clarke. "Social Media Trolls: A Practical Guide for Dealing with Impossible People." Hootsuite blog. February 28, 2019. https://blog.hootsuite.com/how-to-deal-with-trolls-on-social-media/.

3. American Library Association. "ALA Awards 2017 Diversity Research Grants." June 7, 2017. http://www.ala.org/news/press-releases/2017/06/ala-awards-2017-diversity-research-grants.

4. Lisa Peet. "Defeating Bullies and Trolls in the Library Conference Examines Harassment, Doxxing." *Library Journal*. April 25, 2019. https://www.libraryjournal.com/?detailStory=defeating-bullies-and-trolls-in-the-library-conference-examines-harassment-doxxing.

5. Phil Morehart. "Bullying, Trolling, and Doxxing, Oh My! Librarians Tell Stories of Harassment by Conservative Groups." *American Libraries*. June 25, 2018. https://americanlibrariesmagazine.org/blogs/the-scoop/bullying-trolling-doxxing-oh/.

6. April Hathcock. "Post-ALA Race Fatigue." *At the Intersection* blog. June 27, 2017. https://aprilhathcock.wordpress.com/2017/06/27/post-ala-race-fatigue/.

7. Stacy Collins. "Anti-Oppression: Anti-Oppression." Simmons University Library website. Accessed August 8, 2019. https://simmons.libguides.com/anti-oppression.

8. Elvia Arroyo-Ramirez. "Trolls Gonna Troll: When Online Doxxers (Try to) Come Get You." *Medium.* July 3, 2018. https://medium.com/librarieswe here/trolls-gonna-troll-when-online-doxxers-try-to-come-get-you-971367154 2b2.

9. Ibid.

10. Phil Morehart. "Defeating Bullies and Trolls: Skokie (Ill.) Public Library Event Offers Strategies to Protect Librarians from Harassment." *American Libraries.* March 15, 2019. https://americanlibrariesmagazine.org/blogs/the-scoop/librarians-defeating-bullies-trolls/.

11. Morehart, "Bullying, Trolling, and Doxxing, Oh My!"

12. Lara Ewen. "Target: Librarians: What Happens When Our Work Leads to Harassment—or Worse." *American Libraries.* June 3, 2019. https://americanlibrariesmagazine.org/2019/06/03/target-librarians-harassment-doxxing/.

13. ADL, *The Trolls Are Organized.*

14. Zeynep Tufekci. *Twitter and Tear Gas: The Power and Fragility of Networked Protest*, p. 176. New Haven and London: Yale University Press, 2017.

15. Tufekci, 177–78.

16. Whitney Phillips. *This Is Why We Can't Have Nice Things: Mapping the Relationship between Online Trolling and Mainstream Culture.* London: The MIT Press, 2015.

17. Ibid., 10.

18. Ibid., 43.

19. Pierluigi Paganini. "Trolling, Doxing & Cyberstalking: Cybercrime & the Law." Security Affairs. March 3, 2017. https://securityaffairs.co/wordpress/56841/laws-and-regulations/trolling-doxing-cyberstalking-cybercrime-law.html.

20. Phillips, *This Is Why We Can't Have Nice Things*, 153.

21. See, for example, John Cassidy. "Donald Trump Will Go Down in History as the Troll-in-Chief." *The New Yorker.* June 29, 2017. https://www.newyorker.com/news/john-cassidy/donald-trump-will-go-down-in-history-as-the-troll-in-chief; Poppy Noor. "Trump's Troll-in-Chief? Once Again, Nancy Pelosi Bites Back." *The Guardian.* October 17, 2019. https://www.theguardian.com/us-news/2019/oct/17/nancy-pelosi-trump-meeting-photo-meltdown-battle; and Wallace Hettle. "Donald Trump: Troll-in-Chief." History News Network, Columbian College of Arts & Sciences, The George

Washington University. September 19, 2018. https://historynewsnetwork.org/article/169800.

22. EJ Montini. "Donald Trump's Twitter Trolling of Teen Activist Greta Thunberg Should Be Impeachable." *AZ Central.* December 12, 2019. https://www.azcentral.com/story/opinion/op-ed/ej-montini/2019/12/12/donald-trumps-trolling-teen-greta-thunberg-should-impeachable/4417453002/.

23. Phillips, *This Is Why We Can't Have Nice Things*, 25.

24. Ibid., 27.

25. Nate Silver. "Donald Trump Is the World's Greatest Troll." FiveThirtyEight. July 20, 2015. https://fivethirtyeight.com/features/donald-trump-is-the-worlds-greatest-troll/.

26. Brent Bambury. "'They're Trolling the Trolls Back': How Parkland Survivors Are Responding to Conspiracy Theorists." CBC Radio. Accessed December 20, 2019. https://www.cbc.ca/radio/day6/episode-378-school-shooting-conspiracies-olympic-stadiums-rip-arthur-black-a-i-jobs-martin-amis-and-more-1.4546905/they-re-trolling-the-trolls-back-how-parkland-survivors-are-responding-to-conspiracy-theorists-1.4546938.

27. Paganini, "Trolling, Doxing & Cyberstalking."

28. Reeves Wiedeman. "The Sandy Hook Hoax." *New York*. September 5, 2016. http://nymag.com/intelligencer/2016/09/the-sandy-hook-hoax.html.

29. Matthew Schwartz. "Facebook Bans Alex Jones, Louis Farrakhan and Other 'Dangerous' Individuals." NPR. May 3, 2019. https://www.npr.org/2019/05/03/719897599/facebook-bans-alex-jones-louis-farrakhan-and-other-dangerous-individuals.

30. David Hogg and Lauren Hogg. #*NeverAgain: A New Generation Draws the Line*, p. 99. New York: Random House, 2018.

31. Elizabeth Weise. "Online Haters Are Targeting Greta Thunberg with Conspiracy Theories and Fake Photos." *USA Today*. October 2, 2019. https://www.usatoday.com/story/news/nation/2019/10/02/climate-change-activist-greta-thunberg-targeted-online-trolls/3843196002/.

32. Ibid.

33. Patrisse Cullors. "Online Hate Is a Deadly Threat. When Will Tech Companies Finally Take It Seriously?" CNN. November 1, 2018. https://www.cnn.com/2018/11/01/opinions/social-media-hate-speech-cullors/index.html.

34. Philip Napoli. *Social Media and the Public Interest: Media Regulation in the Disinformation Age.* New York: Columbia University Press, 2019.

35. Ibid., 159.

36. Ibid., 175.

37. Patrisse Khan-Cullors and Asha Bandele. *When They Call You a Terrorist: A Black Lives Matter Memoir*, p. 253. New York: St. Martin's Press, 2017.

38. DeRay Mckesson. "'I Learned Hope the Hard Way': On the Early Days of Black Lives Matter." *The Guardian*. April 12, 2019. https://www.theguardian.com/world/2019/apr/12/black-lives-matter-deray-mckesson-ferguson-protests.

39. Hannah Alper. *Momentus: Small Acts, Big Change*, p. 213. Toronto: Nelson Education, 2017.

40. Weise, "Online Haters."

41. Samantha Adams Becker. Interview by Paul Signorelli. April 12, 2018.

42. Maurice Coleman. Interview by Paul Signorelli. April 10, 2018.

43. David Lee King. Interview by Paul Signorelli. April 12, 2018.

44. Becker interview.

11. ORGANIZING TO CHANGE THE WORLD

1. Black Lives Matter. "About Black Lives Matter." Accessed January 5, 2020. https://blacklivesmatter.com/about/.

2. Global Climate Strike. "About Global Climate Strike." Accessed January 5, 2020. https://globalclimatestrike.net/about/.

3. Fridays for Future. "About Fridays For Future." Accessed January 5, 2020. https://www.fridaysforfuture.org/about.

4. Fridays for Future. "Events." Accessed January 5, 2020. https://fridaysforfuture.org/events/map.

5. Center for American Progress. "More Than 1,400 Organizations and Individuals Voice Their Support for DACA." November 7, 2019. https://www.americanprogress.org/issues/immigration/news/2019/11/07/476945/1400-organizations-individuals-voice-support-daca/.

6. March for Our Lives. "Our Mission." Accessed January 5, 2020. https://marchforourlives.com/mission-story/.

7. Me Too. "Healing: Resource Library." Accessed January 6, 2020. https://metoomvmt.org/healing.

8. Just Be Inc. "About Us." Accessed January 6, 2020. https://justbeinc.wixsite.com/justbeinc/purpose-mission-and-vision.

9. Women's March. "Mission and Principles." Accessed January 5, 2020. https://womensmarch.com/mission-and-principles.

10. Dave Cullen. *Parkland: Birth of a Movement*. New York: HarperCollins, 2019.

11. David Hogg and Lauren Hogg. *#NeverAgain: A New Generation Draws the Line*. New York: Random House, 2018.

12. Wikipedia. "School Strike for Climate." Accessed January 5, 2020. https://en.wikipedia.org/wiki/School_strike_for_the_climate.

13. Greta Thunberg. @gretathunberg. Accessed January 6, 2020. https://twitter.com/GretaThunberg.

14. Ibid., Greta Thunberg. Fridays for Future #Climate Strike. Accessed January 6, 2020. https://www.facebook.com/groups/1359887447497383/.

15. Ibid., @gretathunberg. Accessed January 6, 2020. https://www.instagram.com/gretathunberg/?hl=en.

16. Paul Herrera. "Fridays for Future: The Social Media Impact of Greta Thunberg." September 9, 2019. http://mavenroad.com/fridaysforfuture-the-social-media-impact-of-greta-thunberg/.

17. Steven Melendez. "Here's a List of Gun Control Laws Passed Since the Parkland Shooting." *Fast Company.* February 14, 2019. https://www.fastcompany.com/90306582/heres-a-list-of-gun-control-laws-passed-since-the-parkland-shooting.

18. Katherine Schaeffer. "Share of Americans Who Favor Stricter Gun Laws Has Increased Since 2017." Pew Research Center. October 16, 2019. https://www.pewresearch.org/fact-tank/2019/10/16/share-of-americans-who-favor-stricter-gun-laws-has-increased-since-2017/.

19. Joseph Lyons. "How March for Our Lives Wants to Take Its Momentum to the Ballot Box." *Bustle.* March 24, 2018. https://www.bustle.com/p/what-is-vote-for-our-lives-the-march-wants-to-take-its-momentum-to-the-ballot-box-8595931.

20. Charlotte Alter, Suyin Haynes, and Justin Worland. "Time 2019 Person of the Year: Greta Thunberg." *Time.* December 23/30, 2019. https://time.com/person-of-the-year-2019-greta-thunberg/.

21. Damian Carrington. "School Climate Strikes: 1.4 Million People Took Part, Say Campaigners." *The Guardian.* March 19, 2019. https://www.theguardian.com/environment/2019/mar/19/school-climate-strikes-more-than-1-million-took-part-say-campaigners-greta-thunberg.

22. #etmooc. "About." Accessed January 6, 2020. http://etmooc.org/sample-page/.

23. ShapingEDU. "ShapingEDU Live." YouTube. Accessed January 6, 2020. https://www.youtube.com/playlist?list=PLuNZu15Jz9C9hMqHId0qsuZTb4fCl0vPb.

24. Ibid. "2020 ShapingEDU Unconference." Accessed January 6, 2020. https://shapingedu.asu.edu/2020-unconference.

25. Elders Action Network. "Elders Action Network: One Earth, One Humanity, One Future." Accessed January 6, 2020. https://eldersaction.org/.

26. Peter Block. *Community: The Structure of Belonging.* San Francisco: Berrett-Koehler, 2008.

27. John McKnight and Peter Block. *The Abundant Community: Awakening the Power of Families and Neighborhoods*. San Francisco: Berrett-Koehler, 2010.

28. Abundant Community. "Awakening the Power of Families and Neighborhoods." Accessed January 7, 2020. https://www.abundantcommunity.com.

29. ShapingEDU. *Building Effective Communities of Practice* [v3.0]. December 2019. https://shapingedu.asu.edu/communities-of-practice.

30. ShapingEDU. "Building Effective Communities of Practice." YouTube. July 17, 2019. https://www.youtube.com/watch?v=MI6fwO8wpsY& list=PLuNZu15Jz9C9hMqHId0qsuZTb4fCl0vPb&index=13&t=0s.

31. ShapingEDU. *Building Effective Communities of Practice [v3.0]*. https://shapingedu.asu.edu/communities-of-practice-authors.

32. Jen Schradie. *The Revolution That Wasn't: How Digital Activism Favors Conservatives*. Cambridge: Harvard University Press, 2019.

33. Natasha Pinon. "How to Ensure Your Online Activism Has an Offline Impact." *Mashable*. December 3, 2019. https://mashable.com/article/activism-on-social-media/.

34. Schradie, *The Revolution That Wasn't*, 19.

REFERENCES

CHAPTER I: WHAT IS SOCIAL MEDIA AND WHAT CAN IT DO FOR YOU?

Diffusion of Innovations, 5th edition, by Everett Rogers
Fake News, Propaganda, and Plain Old Lies: How to Find Trustworthy Information in the Digital Age, by Donald Barclay
Net Smart: How to Thrive Online, by Howard Rheingold
Social Media for Social Good: A How-to Guide for Nonprofits, by Heather Mansfield
Tweets and the Streets: Social Media and Contemporary Activism, by Paolo Gerbaudo
Twitter and Tear Gas: The Power and Fragility of Networked Protest, by Zeynep Tufekci
Wikipedia: "List of Social Networking Websites," accessed January 16, 2020, https://en.wikipedia.org/wiki/List_of_social_networking_websites; "List of Virtual Communities with More Than One Million Users," accessed January 16, 2020, https://en.wikipedia.org/wiki/List_of_virtual_communities_with_more_than_1_million_users; "Social Media," accessed January 16, 2020, "Social Media," https://en.wikipedia.org/wiki/Social_media; "Social Network," accessed January 16, 2020, https://en.wikipedia.org/wiki/Social_network; "Social Networking Service," accessed January 16, 2020, https://en.wikipedia.org/wiki/Social_networking_service; and "Social Network Hosting Service," accessed January 16, 2020, https://en.wikipedia.org/wiki/Social_network_hosting_service.

CHAPTER 2: THE PROS AND CONS OF FACEBOOK

"Facebook" article on Wikipedia
"How the Facebook Algorithm Works + 5 Best Practices [2020]," by Greg Swan
Facebook for Dummies, 6th edition, by Carolyn Abram
Facebook, "Help Center"

CHAPTER 3: TWITTER—SMALL MESSAGES WITH LARGE RESULTS

"Are Hashtags Still #Relevant for Your Digital Ad Content in 2020?," by Jacquelyn Jacobsma
The Backchannel: How Audiences Are Using Twitter and Social Media and Changing Presentations Forever, by Cliff Atkinson
"Twitter" article on Wikipedia
Twitter for Dummies, 2nd ed., by Laura Fitton, Michael E. Gruen, and Leslie Poston, with a foreword by Jack Dorsey
Twitter, "Help Center"
"The Ultimate Guide to Hosting a Tweet Chat," by Steve Cooper

CHAPTER 4: TAPPING INTO BUSINESS NETWORKS

"Effective Use of Slack," by Jessica Kerr
"How to Use Slack Effectively: 25 Slack Settings and Features That Will Save Your Focus," by Jory MacKay
LinkedIn, "Help Center"
"LinkedIn: Key Principles and Best Practices for Online Networking & Advocacy by Nonprofit Organizations," by Andrew M. Calkins
Slack, "Help Center"
"28 Best Slack Alternatives [in 2020] for Team Communication (You Cannot Live Without)," by Vartika Kashyap

CHAPTER 5: PICTURING CHANGE

"Creative Commons," "Flickr," "Instagram," and "Snapchat" articles on Wikipedia
"5 Arab Activists Using Instagram to Push for Change," by Sarah Ben Romdane, for *Mille* (newsletter)
"How *Seventeen* Is Using Snapchat to Give Young Activists a Voice," by Kayleigh Barber, for *Folio*
"Infopics," by Tony Vincent
Protests, Political Art, Democracy, Social Change group on Flickr

CHAPTER 6: BLOGGING FOR SOCIAL CHANGE

"Blogging for Social Change & Impact: PCDN Resource Guide," from the Peace and Collaborative Development Network
"Draft Blogger's Code of Conduct," by Tim O'Reilly
"How to Choose the Best Blogging Platform in 2020 (Compared)," by *wpbeginner* editorial staff
Wikipedia, "Blog"

CHAPTER 7: BROADCASTS AND PODCASTS

"How to Start Your Own Podcast," by Patrick Allan and Emily Long, on lifehacker.com (posted June 5, 2020, https://lifehacker.com/how-to-start-your-own-podcast-1709798447)
"Inspiring Social Change on Your Channel," by the YouTube Creator Academy
"YouTube Creators Academy" site, with numerous courses designed to help you create, use, and manage a YouTube channel

CHAPTER 8: VIDEOCONFERENCING AND TELEPRESENCE

Building Online Learning Communities: Effective Strategies for the Virtual Classroom (Second Edition), by Rena Palloff and Keith Pratt
Speak for a Living, by Anne Bruce and Sardék Love
Wikipedia, "Cloud-Based Video Conferencing"
Wikipedia, "Telepresence"
Wikipedia, "Videotelephony"

CHAPTER 9: FOLLOW THE MONEY

Fundraising for Social Change, 7th edition, by Kim Klein
"GoFundMe Help Center," accessed May 6, 2019, https://support.gofundme.com/hc/en-us
Hank Rosso's Achieving Excellence in Fundraising, 2nd edition, edited by Eugene R. Tempel
Parkland: Birth of a Movement, by Dave Cullen
"7 Nonprofit Fundraising Books Your Organization Must Read," by Nick Morpus (Capterra's *Fundraising Software* blog; April 11, 2018; https://blog.capterra.com/7-nonprofit-fundraising-books-your-organization-must-read/

CHAPTER 10: FACING INCIVILITY

"How to Handle and Prevent Online Harassment," by Panda Security, February 4, 2019; https://www.pandasecurity.com/mediacenter/panda-security/how-to-handle-online-harassment/
"Social Media Trolls: A Practical Guide for Dealing with Impossible People," by Todd Clarke
"Trolling, Doxing & Cyberstalking: Cybercrime & the Law," by Pierluigi Paganini, March 3, 2017
The Trolls Are Organized and Everyone's a Target: The Effects of Online Hate and Harassment, by ADL (Anti-Defamation League) with Danya Glabau and Jordan Kramer

CHAPTER 11: ORGANIZING TO CHANGE THE WORLD

The Abundant Community: Awakening the Power of Families and Neighborhoods, by John McKnight and Peter Block
Community: The Structure of Belonging, by Peter Block

"Four Tips for Using Social Media in Your Activism," by Alaina Leary, https://www.yesmagazine.org/democracy/2018/04/23/yes-social-media-can-be-used-for-positive-change/

#HashtagActivism: Networks of Race and Gender Justice, by Sarah Jackson, Moya Bailey, and Brooke Foucault Welles

"How to Ensure Your Online Activism Has an Offline Impact," by Natasha Pinon

The Revolution That Wasn't: How Digital Activism Favors Conservatives, by Jen Schradie

INDEX

ABOUT THE AUTHOR

Paul Signorelli is a San Francisco–based writer, trainer/facilitator, presenter, social media strategist, and consultant. He works to foster positive change through innovations in lifelong learning, nurturing face-to-face and online communities and more effectively incorporating technology into work and play—with a strong emphasis on people at the center of endeavors and technology as a tool. He is actively involved in the Association for Talent Development (ATD), American Library Association (ALA), ShapingEDU, and a variety of other organizations, learning communities, communities of practice, and initiatives.

Signorelli continues to design and facilitate face-to-face and online courses, onsite workshops, and webinars. He co-wrote *Workplace Learning and Leadership* (ALA, 2011) and writes for a variety of publications and blogs, including his *Building Creative Bridges* blog (http://buildingcreativebridges.wordpress.com). He can be reached at paul@paul signorelli.com.